Building Profits Through Organizational Change

Building Profits Through Organizational Change

Roger J. Howe

A Division of American Management Associations

Library of Congress Cataloging in Publication Data

Howe, Roger J.
    Building profits through organizational change.

    Includes index.
    1. Organizational behavior. 2. Management.
3. Organizational change. I. Title.
HD58.7.H68   658.4'06   80-69682
ISBN 0-8144-5681-2   AACR2

First Printing

Acknowledgments

I am especially grateful to Fred Cardina for helping me think through many of the ideas in this writing; to Mitchell Fein for permitting me to use his productivity sharing concepts; to Dr. Mark Mindell for helping me develop the survey methods referred to in Chapters 6, 9, and 12; and to Alfred Norwood for contributing to my understanding of strategic planning.

The ideas and solutions of many of my staff members and colleagues from education and industry have greatly enhanced my understanding of how to apply the behavioral science to organizational issues. This book is dedicated to those participants.

Contents

1

Future challenges and the need for organization behavior

THE CHALLENGES of the future to modern business have been well stated by Peter F. Drucker in his book *The Age of Discontinuity.** Drucker indicated that the vast number of changes that are now upon us have created discontinuity in our age and that the most important change is that ". . . knowledge has become the central capital, the cost center, and the critical resource of the economy." Major changes in the workforce, in methods of teaching and learning, in motivational practices, and in the management process itself are outgrowths of these changes. Consequently, changes in virtually all organizational systems and practices have become necessary rather than merely convenient.

To keep abreast of the accelerated pace of learning, organizations have expended a great amount of time and money in disciplines that will help them manage the technical, financial, and human resources of the corporation. New departments with specialized titles such as acquisitions, new business development, operations analysis and research, and human resource development

* New York: Harper & Row, 1969.

have been created in response to declining product life cycles, tougher competition from domestic and distant geographic areas, increased government controls, changes in the workforce, and other outside influences. Faster paced operations, greater numbers of alternatives, growing complexity, and greater dependency on specialization are some characteristics of managing in today's environment. More than ever there is a disturbing probability that sound traditional management, a good market, adequate financing, and good competitive products and services will not necessarily ensure the success of the business. Knowing how to manage in today's environment is subject to continuous updating and improvement.

The growing number of changes within formal bureaucratic organizations has created a time compression. Much less time is available for making insightful decisions and for making the effort necessary to document these decisions. The quickening pace of activity requires a more responsive planning system. Newer technologies require changes in organizational roles and structure and a need for new talents, relationships, and operating philosophy. Teamwork, not new as a concept and often seen as a convenience, is now a necessity for marshaling diverse, specialized talent. More attention is being paid to assessing attitudes, because declining motivation and morale often attend the installation or extension of newer technologies. Critical or periodic shortages of necessary talent are forcing companies to look closely, some for the first time, at internal resource development; the ability to do a better job with existing personnel constitutes a continuing need. Fear of the unknown, the comforts of doing things the "old way," conflicts between resisters and promoters of change are among the many factors that must be managed as changes are introduced into organizations at an accelerated pace.

Carl Rogers, a noted behavioral psychologist, made the observation in 1968 that man's greatest problem in our swiftly changing technological era will be to understand and adapt to continuous change. Yet a surprising number of firms have relied on self-development, casual routines, or no routines for updating supervisory, managerial, and professional personnel to manage changes in technology. When organizations have installed staff functions to train and develop managers, they often confine themselves to traditional educational concepts and specializations. Many of the people doing the training focus on individual skills and behavior rather than on the skill and behavior of the organization as a whole. Therefore, they often exclude important principles related to the way people behave before, during, and after change.

To ready themselves for the opportunities and problems of our rapidly changing world, organizations will have to increase both the effectiveness of their managers and their methods for bringing about needed changes in organizational systems and practices. This book has been written to help managers understand how to manage the process of change by employing proven principles and methods from the field of organization behavior. Organizations cannot change successfully unless the people in them want to change or are willing to accept management's perceptions for change.

The field of organization behavior has grown tremendously in the past fifty years but only in the last decade has it begun to be recognized as a discipline that can contribute to an organization's profitability. The prospects for growth appear to be encouraging as more and more organizations are creating departments and employing highly skilled practitioners to solve their problems.

But in spite of great strides in the field, many organization behavior theories and practices have not been well integrated into ongoing business systems and practices. The overemphasis on group dynamics, interpersonal relations, sensitivity training, career planning, personal counseling, and other psychological and sociological methods has caused many executives to question the value of the discipline—perhaps rightly. Many of the theories have been developed and tested by people in the behavioral sciences in controlled laboratory situations rather than in the business-world setting. Furthermore, most of the contributions to the field have been made by behavioral scientists, who are often perceived as theoretical in approach, and too far removed from the management process.

Perhaps one of the more vivid examples of this point is the current preoccupation with behavior modification that is based on B. F. Skinner's stimulus-response experiments conducted in laboratories with mice, pigeons, rats, and other animals. Although few would question the merits of behavior modification with animals, many doubt its applicability to the complex issues surrounding the study of human behavior.

Definitions of organization behavior abound in textbooks written for the academic community. Research findings occupy page after page in numerous scholarly journals devoted to the study of human behavior in organizations. However, all the writings and research have yet to define organization behavior in terms that are meaningful to those outside the discipline. Even more important, there is a glaring absence of writings that discuss the contributions organization behavior practitioners can make to the profitability of a business concern.

Organization Behavior Defined

Many operating managers are attempting to learn more about the behavioral aspects involved in running the day-to-day affairs of the business, but more often than not they are bewildered by the implications of the term "organization behavior." Some equate the term with the corporation's personnel function. For others, organization behavior signifies sensitivity training, group problem solving, or organization development. And for still others, organization behavior is associated with academic education programs offered in colleges and universities.

But it is clear that an academic approach will not solve business problems. To lay the groundwork for a valid alternative, it is necessary to take a few steps backward in history and outline the theoretical basis that helped to shape contemporary organization behavior practices. Two perspectives—frequently referred to as "scientific management" and "human relations"—can be linked to form a convenient historical chain reaching from the early industrial engineers' view of behavior to that of the current behavioral scientists.

Scientific management perspective

Without doubt, Frederick W. Taylor was most instrumental in helping to shape "classical" or traditional organization theory, which based its managerial philosophy on the idea that most people have to be coerced, controlled, directed, and threatened in order to get them to work toward the achievement of organizational objectives. In keeping with this philosophy, it was not uncommon for management to seek out managers who exhibited certain physical and personality traits that would enable them to study the character, nature, and performance of each worker with a view to finding out his limitations and his possibilities for development.

Other writers such as Max Weber, a sociologist, further shaped the scientific management perspective. Although there were differences in degree and in emphasis between Weber and Taylor, their ideas did converge on several key assumptions; these have been instrumental in shaping both traditional and contemporary management behavior. Influenced by the scientific determinism of the nineteenth century, these men believed that an organization should behave like a machine. Any deviation from a predetermined course of action was charged to either an engineering deficiency or human inadequacy.

The structure of the organization, the assignment of roles, the determination of wages, and the establishment of relationships were all designed by a specialist (ideally an industrial engineer), much in the same way a machine would be designed. All organization policies and practices, it was reasoned, should be based on the dictates of science. Thus, it was necessary to establish work standards for each employee in a scientific manner and to regulate productivity and profit accordingly. Exponents of the scientific management perspective advanced the following positions:

The overall goal of the organization is profit.

Employees work for the organization and should be concerned about making a profit.

Concern for employee satisfaction is always subordinate to concern for profit.

The key determinants of employee effectiveness are task accomplishment, loyalty, and commitment to the organization's goals.

Human relations perspective

In the 1930s there was a distinctive shift in thinking about organizations. In contrast to the scientific management perspective, the human relationists, led by such writers as Elton Mayo and his associates at the Harvard Business School, proposed that organization theory concentrate on worker attitudes, ideas, perceptions, and feelings. This view was based on the idea that people could be motivated to increase their productivity once certain of their psychological and sociological needs were satisfied. The task of the manager, it was argued, is to establish a sense of community within the organization and to promote wide participation in the decision-making process, a sense of mutual confidence and trust between manager and worker, communications within and between organizational units, and the growth and development of people into areas of greater responsibility.

The focus of this movement shifted the attention from the needs of the organization to the needs of the individual and the

Table 1. Comparison of management perspectives.

	Scientific Management	Human Relations
Emphasis	Legalism	Psychosocial needs
Orientation	Task	Relationships
Methods	Work rules Efficiency standards Management controls	Counseling Group decisions Interpersonal trust

group. Those who advocated the human relations approach reasoned that:

The overall goal of the organization is employee satisfaction.

Employees work for the organization but are primarily concerned with their psychological and social needs.

Concern for productivity and profit is subordinate to concern for employee satisfaction.

The key determinants of employee effectiveness can be measured by the human/social conditions that exist in the organization.

Table 1 contrasts the scientific management perspective and the human relations perspective in their approaches to managing. Whereas scientific management relied on legalism and strict adherence to task, the human relations perspective relied on building relationships to sustain and increase the organization's level of productivity.

Organization behavior perspective

In contrast to these two approaches, the organization behavior approach focuses on analyzing behavioral problems associated with the fundamental factors involved in making the business profitable. Thus, its emphasis is on productivity; its orientation is toward tasks and relationships, and its methods are analysis, education, and consultation.

The contemporary view of organization behavior recognizes that:

The overall goals of the company are profit and service to its societies.

Employees work for the company for profit, job satisfaction, and improvements in the quality of their lives.

Concern for employee satisfaction must be displayed until an optimum productivity/satisfaction level is reached.

The key determinants of organizational effectiveness can be measured by the quality and efficiency of products/services produced, the preservation and enhancement of meaningful work, improvements in technology, and profitable growth.

Organization behavior focuses on the yardsticks by which organizations measure their effectiveness in utilizing their technological, financial, and human resources, so practitioners in the field are beginning to tackle a broad range of business problems and opportunities related to strategic planning, organizational structure, staff and line roles, and relationships, teamwork, morale, leadership, and individual behavior. People trained in organization behavior recognize the value of an interdisciplinary approach to understanding and solving business problems; they rely on analytical methods from such fields as sociology, psychology, communication, education, and the management sciences.

Organization behavior, then, might be thought of as an integrating mechanism that brings together multiple disciplines and approaches to analyze problems, assess opportunities, and introduce changes that will enable organizations to respond to the challenge of operating profitability in current and future business environments.

A special knowledge of multiple business functions is required to work in the variety of organizational issues. Practitioners need a blend of skills that bridge the knowledge gap that often exists between the behavioral sciences and the management sciences. The ideal practitioner would be as well rounded as a Renaissance scholar in his knowledge of all organizational functions and as capable as a Roman orator in communicating with any audience on practically any subject.

More realistically, the organization behaviorist should have a demonstrated competency in quantitative methods and research design, organizational structure and job design, group dynamics, management assessment and development, and business planning methodologies. An in-depth knowledge of marketing, employee relations, and management information systems is critical. A basic understanding of all other organizational functions and their relationships is also essential.

In recent years, a number of practitioners have been trained to help solve problems within organizations. Acting as a catalyst, these people attempt to bring together various organization members to analyze and resolve problems within or between departments. Although there is a definite place for this role in organizations, the method is not powerful enough or persuasive enough to affect profitability or to improve the quality of life within the organizations. To be effective, organization behavior must be positioned properly in the structure and must function as an analytical discipline along with other specialized business functions. Just as market and financial analysts analyze business problems and opportunities from marketing and financial perspectives, organization behavior analysts utilize proven methods to analyze business problems and opportunities from a behavioral perspective.

Methods of Analysis

Organization behaviorists can assist management in its attempts to initiate innovations in systems and practices by analyzing both the organization's strengths and its deficiencies. This analysis can be conducted in one of three ways: by analyzing *for* the organization's management, by analyzing *with* the organization's management, or by preparing the organization's management for *self*-analysis.

Analyses for the organization's management are usually conducted by someone outside the work unit being studied, often a consulting firm. In a typical instance members of management are asked to discuss their areas of responsibility, identify problems, and recommend remedial actions. The third party collects the information, assesses implications, and recommends actions. In this approach the role of middle and lower levels of management is limited to that of information provider. They are not involved in analysis of the data collected or in designing recommendations. They are required to implement the recommendations, however, once decisions have been made.

Analyses conducted with the organization's management vary widely in purpose and scope. In some instances, task forces are appointed to work with an analyst to collect and interpret data and to recommend solutions to identified problems. Other approaches range from involving only selected members from specialized staff functions to involving a large number of people in the process. Including managers in the analytical process extends the responsibility for bringing about changes from senior management levels to other levels in the organization's hierarchy. The case studies in Parts I and II detail this approach to organizational studies.

Preparing managers to introduce innovations that are based on an analysis of organizational problems and opportunities without the assistance of a third party (self-analysis) can be achieved through a systematic educational effort. This approach is designed to diffuse the analytical process by encouraging managers to examine the efficiency and effectiveness of their own policies, practices, systems, work outputs, interpersonal relations, and so forth. Chapter 4 provides an in-depth discussion of this approach.

The techniques used by organization behavior practitioners vary widely, and can be applied to macro or micro business problems. The traditional approaches to analyzing business problems as though they were all related to employee morale are heavily supplemented today by a much broader and at the same time more detailed form of analysis. For example, practitioners are now trained to assess the reasons for production problems, increased maintenance costs, excessive turnover, rising workers' compensation claims, and safety deficiencies. Furthermore, they can forecast future manpower requirements by functional area and for the corporation as a whole. They can analyze the company's management resource deficiencies. They can determine organizational problems that lead workers to unionize. They can analyze structural deficiencies and span-of-control problems. They can cause decision bottlenecks and poor management practices to surface.

Organization of the Book

   This book deals primarily with the method of behavioral analysis that can be used to help management plan, organize, and manage in today's environment. The first part of the book discusses the future challenges of managing the corporate planning process. Five major behavioral problems associated with current planning systems are identified and a practical remedy for solving these problems is given. A review of one company's approach to dealing with these problems is presented to illustrate how selected analytical methods from organization behavior can be used to improve the effectiveness of a company's strategic and operational plans.

   Part II outlines various analytical approaches that can be used to examine organizational structure. What should the role of a staff department be? How can staff effectiveness be measured? What are the behavioral implications of reorganizing and resizing operating units? What relationship should exist between structure and strategy? These questions are addressed within the context of an approach that demonstrates how to achieve greater staff and operating efficiencies while reducing corporate overhead expenses at the same time.

Managing employees is an ever-present challenge to management. Part III provides an analytical basis for understanding how work values and managerial styles combine to motivate employees. What job-related values do employees have that can be used as a basis for motivation? How can these values be assessed? Do managers possess superior physical, intellectual, and motivational characteristics that are distinguishable from those of nonmanagers? Do the numerous techniques and development programs serve the fundamental purpose of building effective managers and organizational teamwork? Is there an effective way to measure employee attitudes? Does improving employee satisfaction result in increased profits? By employing the most up-to-date analytical methods, organization behavior practitioners can provide management with enough of a data base to answer these questions and to make decisions on how to manage employees.

The main objective of this book is to present the discipline of organization behavior as a practical means for helping management analyze and remedy organizational problems. In order to make effective use of the principles outlined, the reader must be willing to reconsider many traditional methods of analyzing and resolving business problems.

The concepts and methods presented should be of special interest to the top executive who is looking for the right approaches for introducing changes in the organization that will increase profits and further human values. Managers who wish to keep abreast of some of the latest developments in the field of behavioral management, particularly from an application perspective, will benefit by learning the concepts and applying the approaches suggested. Some may want to use this book in management training and development courses that focus on viewing the organization from a behavioral perspective. Practitioners in the field may find it useful as a resource for their library.

In the past few years, those of us in the behavioral sciences have witnessed a burgeoning of interest in all aspects of organization behavior—theory, research development of new methodologies, and the opening of new positions for practitioners. As the world of business becomes more complex, specialized disciplines must become more interdependent. The discipline of organization behavior cannot solve all the problems that lie ahead for us as managers, but it does present a strategic and analytical approach for improving the profitability of corporations.

Summary

Beginning with Frederick Taylor and the scientific management movement, the behavioral sciences have had both a direct and an indirect impact on the management process. The direct contributions include the development of analytical approaches that provide specific methods for collecting, organizing, and analyzing information related to a number of important organizational factors. Taylor and his followers provided the concepts that eventually led to time-and-motion studies for increasing operating efficiencies, but contemporary behavioral scientists have given us the means for assessing such factors as the effectiveness of organizational structure, the condition of worker attitudes, and the potential for increasing employee motivation.

More important, however, are the indirect contributions the behavioral sciences have made to profitability. The modern manager, faced with a changing workforce, an uncertain environment, and an ever-present need to improve productivity and efficiency levels, has come to realize that motivating the organization's human resource provides the only real hope for the continued survival of the free enterprise system. The emergence of organization behavior has demonstrated that the science of human behavior can be of help in analyzing and prescribing for some of the maladies that affect the human being at work.

By making the manager aware of the insights of the behavioral sciences, we can provide him or her with the concepts and methods required to manage successfully in the rapidly changing business environment.

I

Planning for Increased Profitability

Today we stand at a unique point in time. The growth experienced in the domestic economy from 1950 to 1973 appears to have come full cycle. The almost 25-year history of liberal monetary policy, limited détente, developing world economies, and full employment is over. The rise of the Third World, especially the Middle East, and the concomitant control of natural resources assures future uncertainty about the supply of raw materials. The gradual decay of international monetary systems and fluctuating currency markets signal uncertainty.

At home the ever-present threat of inflation, the prospect of long-term capital shortages, and continued government intervention in the free enterprise system make the domestic economy almost as difficult to forecast as the world economy. The ever-decreasing birthrate in the United States, combined with the uncertainty in both the domestic and world environments, allows only one general statement to be made about the future of the economy: It will definitely not be an extrapolation of the past. We are going to be living in an era of increasing uncertainty, discontinuity, and change.

Traditionally, companies have attempted to manage uncertainty through planning. At best, these efforts have yielded mixed results. It appears that in a large number of companies, planning still tends to be an academic, often ill-defined activity with little or no measurable bottom-line impact.

In the past, highly successful corporations were built and sustained through diversification and financial leverage. In the future, top performing companies will be characterized by a clear sense of purpose and a dedication to improved productivity. Managing change rather than being managed by it will require a strengthening of corporate responsiveness to the environment. This can only be obtained by improving the process by which corporations plan.

Part I first examines the problems that many companies have with their current planning systems and suggests some criteria for evaluating planning effectiveness. Improving the planning process requires a departure from traditional methods. By incorporating selected principles and techniques from the behavioral sciences, which are reviewed in Chapters 2 to 4, it is possible to improve planning productivity.

2

Analyzing
the planning process

PLANNING is a relatively new management technique that has undergone a variety of changes since its first widespread acceptance in business in the 1950s. In this 30-year time span planning has gradually grown to include more and more elements of the management process. What started out as an extension of the budgeting process has grown to include planning systems for finance, personnel, marketing, operations, and other areas. There are, however, innumerable case histories in which company management has been persuaded that a formal planning process is essential—only to find out that the process itself created interdepartmental feuds, compiling of useless information, and a degeneration in the credibility of planning itself.

The age-old task of management—to apply the right resources to the right business efforts—has become increasingly difficult. The traditional management method of getting the corporation through the horns of each dilemma by brute management force will no longer work. In order to exploit change rather than be ex-

This chapter is based in part on an article co-authored by Roger J. Howe and Alfred W. Norwood, "Merging O.D. with Planning as a Response to Change," *Management Review,* June 1976.

ploited by it, management must enhance corporate responsiveness and productivity through improved planning.

In spite of the rapid evolution of planning from the military logistical systems characteristic of the 1930s and 1940s to today's more sophisticated forms of environmental scanning, econometric models, market forecasts, and so forth, the fact remains that most planning systems are not designed for rapidly changing times.

Achieving and sustaining exceptional performance through planning is not easy. According to a May 1978 issue of *Forbes:* "Only seven of the top 20 companies in terms of return on equity in 1971 were among the top 20 companies in 1974. Only two of the top 20 companies in terms of earnings per share growth in 1971 were among the top 20 companies of 1971. Only one of the top 20 companies in stock price gain in 1971 was in the top 20 companies in 1974." Gaining maximum leverage from the corporation's resources should be the function of an effective planning system. However, most planning systems are not responsive to the emerging needs of today's business world, as evidenced by the five following problems.

Structured planning and the unstructured environment

With operational executive management facing an increasing number of problems and opportunities, real pressure often builds to condense the amount of time devoted to planning efforts. This is usually accomplished by requesting updates only of last year's plan, reducing plans to nothing but numbers, or increasing the number of inputs from operating divisions. Paradoxically, at a time when flexible plans are needed more than ever, many corporations' planning efforts have become more structured and, therefore, less responsive. As a result, most corporations back into the future, judging where they are going from where they have been.

Given the amount of uncertainty in tomorrow's environment, corporations must reexamine the nature of their planning effort.

Instead of relying on highly structured planning systems alone, organizations will have to develop more flexible methods of responding to managing change.

Time and timeliness

A second reason planning efforts become more structured is that planning takes too long. By the time experts make their forecasts, staff functions interpret the experts, and operational management interprets the staff's interpretations, it's too late. Plans are usually outdated by the time they are written. To be effective, planning has to be an on-line function. Plans must reflect the probability of the future and the reality of the present. To do so they must be an integral part of the management process. Figure 1 suggests the wide range of operations that have to be taken into account when planning.

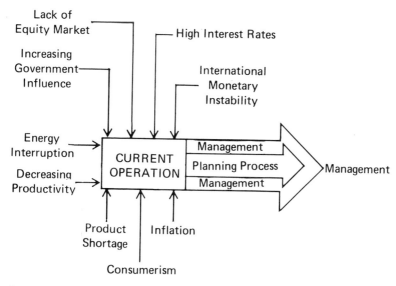

Figure 1. Integrating planning with management.

Corporate stretch and divisional sandbagging

Tying plans and budgets to compensation creates another hurdle for conventional planning systems. Generally, the more entrenched and sophisticated the planning system, the more discretionary income is tied to plans and budgets. Since overachievement is rewarded more than the achievement of plans and budgets, operations management soon realizes that the name of the game is "sandbagging." Recognizing this, managers build stretch into their plans by pressuring operating divisions into overly optimistic commitments.

The following scenario illustrates how a typical discussion between a corporate executive and a division manager can lead to a political settlement that may not reflect business realities.

EXECUTIVE: *Frankly, I was disappointed in your plan. Division A always has to have growth in earnings in excess of 20 percent per year; your plan indicates 10 percent. To be honest, I would like to see a budget in excess of 20 percent next year.*

MANAGER: Sir, the situation has changed since you ran Division A. Earnings in the past were overstated due to a lack of investment in R&D. Not only that, but the economy is off, we're at the bottom of the capital goods cycle, and our competitor has just introduced a new line that damn near obsoletes ours.

EXECUTIVE: *You were made division manager because we knew we could count on you. Despite all the problems, Division A still has great opportunities. I know it and you know it; we are going to count on you for a 15 percent earnings increase next year.*

MANAGER: We will try our best and I am sure we won't disappoint you.

Since such negotiation usually takes place at the end of the planning and/or budgeting cycle, it is almost impossible to translate these political revisions into actions. Because negotiated plans and budgets too often bear little resemblance to reality, they have little credibility and, therefore, little chance for fulfillment.

Corporate and divisional strategy

Another difficulty of current planning systems develops when operating divisions' plans are integrated into a corporate plan. It is customary today to view a corporation as a holding company with a wide variety of operating investments. This concept advocates that each corporate business be viewed in terms of investment and return. The strategic questions deal with which businesses to fund, which businesses to milk, which businesses to sell, and which businesses to purchase. Each business segment is viewed as being on a maturity curve, with position on the curve reflecting its growth potential and funding requirements. While the use of portfolio management strategy greatly facilitates the ease of strategic planning at a corporate level, it tends to obscure the operating reality of each business by reducing strategic concepts to quantitative considerations only.

A holding company or a portfolio manager must review potential performance of alternative investment opportunities on some common base. In a modern multicompany it is extremely likely that the corporate-level numbers, ratios, formats of strategy statements, and so on may reflect this conceptual reality, but they rarely reflect the reality of the operating division's performance. Consequently, changes in the operating plans made at the corporate level and based on corporate strategy may or may not be translated into the implementation of plans at the divisional level, as indicated in Table 2.

Vertical and horizontal planning

A fifth major problem arising from conventional planning deals with the relationship between corporate planning and divi-

Table 2. Corporate and divisional strategy.

			Divisions	
Goals	Corporate	A	B	C
Earnings per share growth	15%	5%	30%	25%
Return on investment	25%	40%	8%	10%
Industry type	High technology	Medium technology	High technology	Low technology
Proprietary positions	Proprietary positions	Nonproprietary positions	Quasi-proprietary positions	Nonproprietary positions
Geographic diversity	Multinational	Multinational	Domestic regional	Domestic

sional planning. We have labeled integration between corporate and divisional plans as vertical planning integration, and the integration of one division's plans with another as horizontal planning integration. All too often a detailed analysis of the operating division's plans shows that human resource plans, marketing plans, and financial plans have been authored by different people, with little or no intradivisional, let alone interdivisional, coordination. In fact, very few companies even recognize this as a problem, because most planning systems actually achieve only a token amount of either type of planning integration. Similarly, an analysis of large or diversified corporate plans frequently reveals that plans are integrated only quantitatively. But today, numbers are not enough. To achieve optimum synergy, management must work toward the goal of integrating the corporation's total planning efforts at the level indicated in Figure 2.

Why the Problems Exist

To understand why these five problems exist, it is essential to understand the perceptions that planners, line managers, and executive managers have toward the planning process itself. Planners typically view themselves as catalysts in the planning process. An old planning axiom states that planners should never do the planning, but instead should encourage and aid line management to do the planning itself. Because line managers are action oriented, they interpret this passivity on the part of the planner as a weakness. They see planners as ineffectual agents who specialize in collecting, but not acting on, information. Planners and their function are, therefore, regarded as being intellectual, aloof, and academic, but not important or effectual.

Since planners' requests do not appear to deal with today's decisions, line management neither feels involved with nor puts a high priority on the planning process and therefore experiences little intellectual or emotional commitment to the resulting plans.

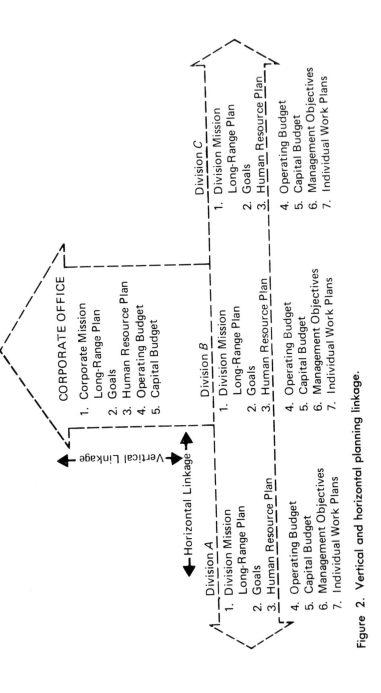

Figure 2. Vertical and horizontal planning linkage.

Consequently, the executive manager is faced with a dilemma. He needs information to help him establish a direction for the corporation. Furthermore, he realizes that he has to organize his management around objectives to assure congruity of effort. In conversations with line management, he ascertains the lack of all-out line commitment to plans. Often the planner presents him with information that is either at the wrong level of detail or insufficient for his needs. He becomes overwhelmed by too many alternative options and decisions, or he is not presented with enough alternatives. As a result, he can offer little commitment to planning itself.

With no commitment to plans, many companies go from crisis to crisis, responding like an amoeba to heat and cold. Conventional planning in most corporations has become a rudder without a ship. Knowing what the problems associated with planning are and knowing why they exist provide the perspective necessary to increase planning productivity. However, to design and implement a productive planning system, it is important to evaluate the effectiveness of the existing system first.

Measuring Planning Effectiveness

In today's economy, every management function has to contribute to the corporation's profit picture. The argument that certain areas of management should be exempt from performance evaluations because their impact on the corporation cannot be measured most certainly does not apply to the planning function. Ineffective planning costs far more than the obvious cost of wasted effort and expense. The difference between the company's actual performance and what the company's performance could have been had planning been better is the larger and more significant measure of planning effectiveness.

If a company's planning effort is nonexistent, weak, or ineffective, it is impossible for management to make the best decisions concerning the future of the corporation. The questions that follow have been designed to aid management with the task of evaluating the company's planning efforts.

Corporate planning range

1. Have previous plans adequately reflected current conditions (product/material scarcity, customer demand, technological advances, production costs, financing constraints, and opportunities)?

2. Are operating alternatives originated, analyzed, and decided upon by the most appropriate personnel?

3. Is corporate strategy stated explicitly and based on thorough consideration of:
   Your public's expectations?
   Your management's aspirations?
   Maximum utilization of capital, human, and
      systems resources?
   Operating divisions' available opportunities
      and constraints?
   Existing company momentum?

4. Is the corporate plan fully integrated with resource allocation, goal-directed budgets, and group/individual work plans?

Corporate planning impact

1. Has planning had an observable or measurable impact on the historical growth of corporate profits?

2. Does each planning exercise begin with an audit of previous planning activity and results?

3. In times of discontinuity (price/wage controls, product shortage, rapid inflation, natural and/or manmade disaster), has the company functioned by contingency plan or reflex?

4. How many of the company's operating divisions had below par performances in the past three years?

5. Have the vast majority of the corporate R&D and market research efforts had tangible positive results?

6. In retrospect, would the company still have made the acquisitions and/or divestitures it made in previous years?

Corporate planning commitment

1. Does operating and staff management have high emotional investment in existing company plans?

2. Is the company's personal plan for the future development of the corporation congruent with the corporate plan?

3. How many big executives or promising managers has the company lost due to disagreement with changes in policy or strategy?

4. Do the company's financial publics (investors, security analysts) and management perceive the same long-range goals and means to achieve those goals?

5. If the company dropped its planning efforts tomorrow, would management be relieved or anxious?

Summary

Today's corporation must place an enormous demand on its planning function. It is only through a fully integrated, responsive planning effort that a company can maximize the prductivity of its capital, human, and systems resources. Commonly understood and agreed-to plans will assure the congruity of management effort, which is the key to organizational success.

How can a company overcome the five planning problems discussed in this chapter? What management techniques can be employed to ensure a positive repsonse to each of the above questions? The next chapter outlines an approach to planning that can be used by management to produce plans that will increase corporate profitability.

3

Improving
the planning process

THE SUCCESS of the corporate planning process depends on the degree of understanding and coordination realized between individuals and work teams. In recent years, some organizations have begun to use selected principles and techniques from the behavioral sciences to improve the effectiveness and efficiency of their planning system. Using techniques such as team planning sessions, in which small groups are brought together to establish personal and/or team development plans, these organizations are attempting to involve more of the company's human resources in the planning process.

However, the potential contribution of the behavioral sciences in the planning process hasn't been realized. Most behavioral planning techniques are designed to help individuals and teams integrate their plans, creative abilities, technical knowledge, and energy with the organization's existing plans. Only in rare instances have these techniques been adapted to make the planning process itself more responsive to the organization's immediate and future development needs.

To illustrate how the planning process can be improved, let's first review three specific techniques that can be integrated into the planning process and then examine how one company resolved its planning problems through the application of some basic principles and techniques from the behavioral sciences.

Delphi Technique

"Project Delphi" was the title of study sponsored by the Air Force and conducted by the Rand Corporation in the early 1950s. The purpose of this study was to solicit expert opinion on the estimated number of A-bombs required to reduce munitions output by a prescribed amount. The method used was to obtain a reliable consensus of opinion from a group of experts by using a series of questionnaires interspersed with controlled opinion feedback.

Through the work of Olaf Helmar, one of the technique's pioneers, the Delphi approach has been expanded. It is now widely used for technological forecasts and social and political trend predictions, and it provides general-purpose methods for obtaining group consensus, solving problems, and forming policy. The technique derives its usefulness from the realization that projections into the future are based largely on the personal expectations of people rather than on scientifically reliable predictions.

Perhaps the simplest and most complete definition of Delphi was offered by A. L. Delbecq, A. H. Van de Ven, and D. H. Gustafson:*

> The Delphi technique is a method for the systematic solicitation and collation of judgments on a particular topic through a set of carefully designed sequential questionnaires interspersed with summarized information and feedback of opinions derived from earlier responses.

The Delphi method follows a simple design:

1. Participants in the process are asked to give their opinions in writing regarding (a) the nature of a problem, (b) possible so-

* *Group Techniques for Program Planning.* Clearview, Ill.: Scott, Foresman, 1975.

lutions to a selected problem, (c) the potential value of a proposed solution, or (d) the future direction of a product or event
or other issues related to a designated topical area.

2. The results from this survey are tabulated and fed back to the
    participants without identification of who has voiced what
    opinions.

3. Participants who deviate from the most favored opinion are
    asked to state anonymously, in writing, their reasons for hold-
    ing that position.

4. This information is fed back to participants and they are again
    asked to state their opinion in writing, based on this additional
    input.

5. These results are tabulated and fed back to the members to-
    gether with concise summaries provided by those who are still
    deviant.

The call for a restatement of opinions with reasons for continued
deviation may be repeated as often as four or five times.

Although the original format of Delphi called for the use of
written surveys and written feedback, the methodology has been
altered successfully by building in other information collection
and dissemination processes (discussed in the case study that follows) that speed up the communication process. There is a good
deal of evidence that the Delphi technique, when tailored to specific informational requirements, can lead toward consensus with
less interpersonal tension than other data collection procedures
that focus only on face-to-face discussion or only on written questionnaires.

Cybernetic Technique

The term "cybernetic" is used to refer to a specific communication process that allows management to generate and organize
information or ideas quickly and effectively in moderate to large

groups. The technique is called "cybernetic" because of the flow of events that take place when it is used. John Hall and Roger Dixon, in their explanation of the process, write that: "Just as the human brain can manage a myriad of complex relationships, and the computer can keep track of and classify a large volume of inputs in an incredibly brief span of time, so the cybernetic session allows us to bundle many variables and a large volume of input into a concise time frame."* The technique works as follows:

1. Classifiy the major topics of an issue or concern into an even number of questions. (The usual procedure is to formulate four major questions.) The questions may overlap, so long as there is enough latitude to permit discussion on any aspect of the larger issue(s).

2. The questions should then be constituted as communication stations where a free form of dialog can take place.

3. Next, a schedule should be drawn up that shows the individual where he or she should be (station) and when, and the major question for the station.

4. A person should be assigned to each station to record data and to review what has been said thus far as new participants arrive at a station. The role of the recorder is to collect, organize, and summarize data. He or she is not to serve as a discussion leader.

By following the preestablished pattern outlined on the itinerary card, participants move from one station to another, interacting with others as both listeners and speakers. At specific time intervals, half the participants at each station will move to a new station. The remaining half continues its discussion, with additional ideas brought into the group from new members. The departing participants do not move as a group but disperse to separate stations. (See Figure 3.)

The advantage of the cybernetic technique is that it enables its users to gather a great deal of information from a large number of

* "Cybernetic Sessions: A Technique for Gathering Ideas," *The 1974 Annual Handbook for Group Facilities.* La Jolla, Calif.: University Associates, 1974.

PARTICIPANT *X*

Period	Station	Period	Station
8:30-9:55	1	8:30-9:55	3
10:00-11:25	4	10:00-11:25	3
11:30-1:00	4	11:30-1:00	1
B r e a k			
2:00-3:25	2		
3:30-5:00	2		

Figure 3. Example of an itinerary card.

people in a relatively short period of time. It can be used in situations in which creative ideas are sought, group problem solving is desirable, large amounts of data are needed on a given subject, or a substitute for written attitude surveys is necessary. Although the original intent of the technique was to gather ideas without evaluation of their worth, the process can be adapted to making evaluations with only slight variation.

Force-Field Analysis Technique

Kurt Lewin, who developed the concept and technique of force-field analysis, maintained that any problem situation is the way it is at any given moment because sets of counterbalancing forces are keeping it that way. The technique of force-field analysis seeks to identify these forces by providing a framework for solving problems, evaluating ideas, or implementing planned changes.

Figure 4 illustrates the Lewin concept. The top and bottom of the figure represent opposite ends of a continuum of a problem; the environmental conditions and pressures pushing to support a favorable condition are the *driving forces* represented by the arrows

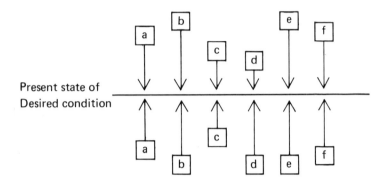

Figure 4. The force field.

pushing upward that, at the same time, act as barriers for preventing unfavorable movement away from the desired state. The arrows pushing downward represent the *restraining forces* that are preventing the achievement of the more desired state.

The group of forces in Figure 4 is called a "force field." The length of the arrows describes the relative strength of the force; the longer the arrow, the stronger the force. Thus, to stabilize behavior, people and organizations work to equalize the strength of the forces. Change will occur only if the forces are modified so that the system can move to a different level, where it can again stabilize itself by equalizing the driving and restraining forces. The equilibrium can be changed by (1) strengthening or adding forces in the direction of change, (2) reducing or moving some of the restraining forces, or (3) changing the direction of the forces.

This technique has been used in numerous situations in which a person or a group is evaluating the likelihood of success or failure of a proposed action. In the illustration that follows, the technique was blended with the cybernetic technique to assess the environmental forces and business conditions that might affect the future direction of a specific company.

Case Study

Recognizing the need for a new approach to guide the corporation's market planning process, the president of a mid-sized manufacturing company formed a problem-solving task force consisting of both line and staff personnel. The task force was commissioned to develop a process that would provide answers to several strategic issues of importance to executive decision making. Guided by the major reason for a new approach, namely, that past approaches for gathering data had not produced reliable information, the task force began by formulating the questions that needed to be answered before specific recommendations could be made to top management.

After an initial discussion of the problems associated with the previous approaches used to gather planning information, the task force concluded that it must address three specific issues related to the five planning problems identified in Chapter 2. The first issue was that past data-gathering procedures were too intricate, detailed, and time consuming. Past suggestions by top management to streamline the process and make it less burdensome had been ignored. The second was that too few individuals were consulted before final conclusions were made and that the people consulted were not necessarily closest to the markets under study. The third issue was that there was frequent second guessing of one division's marketing plan by another division, which usually resulted in major alteration and repackaging of the plans. This problem was responsible for creating major conflicts and mistrust among key managers at both the corporate and the divisional levels.

To address these problem areas, the task force designed a new approach to gathering market data and to moving key managers toward a consensus on the major questions related to the company's strategic market plans. The new approach was designed to broaden the base of input into the strategic plan by including managers and specialists whose position in the organization placed them closest to the information needed to make top management decisions. Since time was of the essence in arriving at a plan to present to the company's board of directors, the task force decided to gather the planning data as quickly as possible so that there would be enough time to analyze alternatives and to prepare a final presentation. After receiving approval from top management, the task force proceeded to gather, analyze, and formulate a marketing plan, using behavioral science principles and methodologies.

Gathering planning data

To avoid the problems associated with most highly structured planning systems and to compress the amount of time usually required to gather and analyze planning data, the task force utilized a modified version of the Delphi technique. It systematically collected and collated the judgments of staff and line managers for formulating answers to the key strategic questions.

To implement the Delphi procedure, the data collection design followed these general procedures: The task force preformulated a questionnaire consisting of a number of obvious financial and organizational issues facing the company, seeding the list with an initial range of options but providing space for respondents to add to the lists. The questionnaire was then administered to a random sample of managers who would not be included in the survey in order to test the clarity and meaningfulness of the information requested.

After a debriefing session with the sample group a revised questionnaire was prepared and administered to a previously agreed-upon participant list. Participants were asked for their position on each item, with a brief explanation of their underlying assumptions. Those participating in this study represented several organizational levels and diverse functional areas. The questionnaire was divided into three parts and required three or four hours of each participant's time.

In Part 1 of the questionnaire participants were asked to respond to a comprehensive list of current and future business problems/opportunities and to revise or add to the preformulated list. In Part 2 the problems and opportunities were prioritized by the participants, using a five-point scale. Where appropriate, participants were asked to rate the degree to which they felt qualified to answer the question. In Part 3 participants were asked to assess the interdependency of priority problems for which shifts in priority rankings were obvious and determine which resources, if any, could be applied to the solution of priority problems.

The Delphi design incorporated the essential features of reliable data collection in that it allowed for anonymity, controlled feedback, and statistical analysis of the results.

Analyzing planning data

After collecting and prioritizing the data, the task force used the cybernetic technique to analyze the data further to gain mutual input from key operating and staff management. This was accomplished by bringing together fifteen of the company's top executives for a two-day time period. After an initial in-depth review of the data from the Delphi surveys and some factual data prepared by the task force, the large group was broken up into small groups that were asked to discuss the major areas of agreement and disagreement further. These groups were asked to consider alternative strategic scenarios that had been designed by the task force after the Delphi survey. As indicated in the description of the cybernetic technique, the participants rotated through each of the groups in different participant configurations. Individual members of the task force acted as recorders for each of the small group meetings.

The input from these discussions was then summarized and fed back to the large group by the recorders. Since a great deal of information had been gathered in a relatively small amount of time, only the major points of agreement, disagreement, or analysis were fed back at this time. At the conclusion of the feedback session the group agreed that it had developed a fuller understanding of the company's problems and future opportunities.

The fact that a large number of random thoughts and assumptions had been heard and tested by the key decision makers in the company led the group to the conclusion that the cybernetic process served both as an educational experience and as an invaluable mechanism for self-expression and listening to the views of others. Furthermore, because they had the opportunity to receive instant feedback and to influence each other's views in a free form of dialog, the group took on the complexion of a problem-solving team; each member felt integrally involved and "in" on information and decisions vital to the future of the business. And top management felt that it had an invaluable source of data from the people in the organization who were in the best position to influence the decision that had to be made.

Implementing the plan

After the cybernetic session, the large group drafted a final copy of the marketing plan and developed the procedures for obtaining additional involvement from operating managers. These managers, after all, would ultimately have to implement the programs and policies necessary to achieve the growth objectives identified in the plan. Because involvement at the implementation stage is equally as important as it is in the data-gathering and analytical stages, several key managers who participated in the group discussions were charged with the responsibility of communicating the plan downward in the organization. Using a structured format, the company's president gave the group the specific assignment of

Statement of Policy or Strategy:

_____

_____

On a scale of 1 (low) to 5 (high), what in your opinion is the relative strength of the force?

Positive Forces	**Restraining Forces**
Strength	Strength
_____A	_____A
_____B	_____B
_____C	_____C
_____D	_____D
_____E	_____E
_____F	_____F
_____G	_____G
_____H	_____H
_____I	_____I

Positive Forces
Events or conditions internal or external to the company that will push the policy/strategy forward.

Restraining Forces
Events of conditions internal or external to the company that will act as barriers to forward movement of the strategy.

Figure 5. Force-field analysis.

evaluating the proposed plan, using the force-field analysis technique. Figure 5 is an example of the format used by the group in assessing the forces they felt would contribute to achieving or blocking the objectives detailed in the plan.

When the group finished its analysis, the recorders again summarized (quantitatively and qualitatively) the input from the participants. They fed this information back to the group the same day. Action plans were developed to take advantage of the positive forces and to counter the impact of the restraining forces.

Behavioral Science Principles

The key to improving the corporate planning process is for top management to recognize that gaining understanding and commitment to plans requires broad participation at the data-gathering, data-analysis, and implementation phases. Managers should have a part in shaping the plans they have been asked to implement. In the preceding example, management discovered that the most effective way to address the planning problems referred to in Chapter 2 is to include the key management group in the planning process.

Utilizing selected group process techniques makes it possible to involve many managers in the total process. The application of these techniques can make planning more efficient by gaining group consent at each phase of the process. It is particularly important that plans not only be formulated using group process techniques, but that they also be communicated downward. Clarification of and input into plans by those who must carry them out are essential requisites to commitment.

In asserting that the planning process can be improved by expanding the number of participants involved in the process, I have made the following assumptions, which William Gordon and I documented in *Team Dynamics in Developing Organizations.**

* The creativity, competence, and knowledge required to formulate corporate plans are distributed widely in an organization.

* Dubuque, Iowa: Kendall/Hunt Publishing, 1977.

- A group of individuals can produce higher quality solutions than one person when tasks are complex, unprogrammed, and unusual.
- A group approach to collecting and analyzing information and to formulating and implementing plans and actions will generate a higher accuracy and quality of plans than those generated by individuals working alone.
- Involving more managers in the planning process will increase the intellectual and emotional commitment to the final product—the plans themselves.

In today's business environment it is increasingly evident that planning the corporation's destiny does not lend itself to precise analytical techniques. Rather, most planning efforts benefit from the subjective judgments of people of diverse experience and expertise.

Summary

In the previous chapter, I indicated that conventional planning is often viewed as a passive discipline because it leaves the implementation of plans to other functions. In this chapter I have suggested that applying selected techniques from the behavioral sciences could improve the planning process. By using group-dynamic information-collecting techniques such as the Delphi approach, cybernetics, and force-field analysis, more of the company's resources can participate in a constructive way in helping to design as well as implement the company's plans.

Increasing the number of participants in the planning process makes it possible to close the gap between planning and action. By expanding participation in the total process, management decreases the amount of time required to implement programs and policies designed to realize plans. Through the application of behavioral science principles and techniques, the five problems experienced by conventional planning become manageable.

In the next chapter we will explore in greater detail an approach that can be used to implement change both in the planning process itself and in the organization that must support corporate plans.

4

Implementing change in the planning process

ADVOCATES of the scientific management perspective were quite explicit in their view that innovation could only be accomplished by a select group of elite managers and technical experts. Now, however, we know that it is possible for people at multiple levels in an organizational hierarchy to collaborate in analyzing and introducing changes in technology, structure, management style, and the planning process itself. We also know that these changes can have dramatic impact on the corporation's balance sheet.

Broadening the number of people involved in analyzing problems and opportunities can create an atmosphere of distrust, anxiety, and even open hostility, unless the organization is properly prepared for "self-analysis." If we extend the analogy that introducing change within an organization requires the same form of analysis as introducing a new product to the market, it follows that the same criteria used to measure the potential success of a product can be applied to changes introduced within an organization.

For a product to be successful in the marketplace it must generally meet five major criteria. First, the individual/organization must believe that the product has an advantage over the product it is replacing. Second, it must be compatible with the potential user's values, past experiences, and needs. Third, it must be seen on a limited basis to ensure its testability. Fourth, the results of using the product must be observable before the product is finally accepted. Fifth, the features and benefits of the product should be viewed as reasonably easy to understand. Before introducing a product to the market, it is therefore essential to analyze potential users in terms of their historical and current trends of acceptance, values, concerns, capacity to change, and related factors.

Organizations can benefit by designing and implementing strategies that incorporate these same criteria for introducing changes within the organization. This chapter discusses a strategy that can be used to expand an organization's capacity for introducing changes in the planning process and in the other organizational policies and practices needed to facilitate the attainment of objectives inherent in the plans themselves.

An Educational Strategy

To be accepted within an organization, a change must be viewed as compatible with both individual and organizational goals. The importance of such compatibility was stated articulately by Jean Jacques Rousseau in *The Social Contract:*

> The problem is to find a form of association that will defend
> and protect with the whole common force the person and
> good of each associate, and in which each, while uniting
> himself with all, may still obey himself alone and remain as
> free as before.

In their famous Hawthorne studies,* F. J. Roethlisberger and W. J. Dickson suggested that management has two major functions: to secure the profitability of the total organization and to secure the "equilibrium of the social organization so that individuals contributing their service to this common purpose obtain personal satisfactions that make them willing to cooperate." Behaviorist

* *Management and the Worker,* Cambridge, Mass.: Harvard University Press, 1939.

Chris Argyris also concerned himself with how an organization can be created in which the individual can obtain maximum expression while "the organization itself may obtain optimum satisfaction of its demands." The International Congress of Applied Psychology devoted an entire conference to a discussion of how people can work together in a manner that will satisfy their needs as well as the objectives of the organization to which they belong. One of the most important conclusions from this conference was that before change can be introduced successfully within an organization, the organization and each employee must feel that they benefit from it.

The compatibility of individual and organizational goals can be achieved by including members from within the organization in the design, analysis, and implementation stages of the innovation. Organizations typically spend a great deal of time and effort training their marketing personnel for sales outside the organization, yet they often neglect to train internal personnel who would be responsible for implementing innovations within the organization. Most research suggests that the acceptance of a change within the organization is directly related to the knowledge and skills of *internal personnel who are in the best position to introduce change* in that they know the system, understand and speak the language of the organization, understand the norms of the organization, identify with the organization's needs and goals, and are familiar with the potential users.

Some companies introduce change in the planning process after training managers and planners within the organization in behavioral science techniques. The principals and techniques learned in the program are transferable to any planning or decision-making process that makes use of a group approach.

The Curriculum

The curriculum, which is accredited by a major university, alternates 6 one-week workshop modules (see Figure 6) with normal

Figure 6. Program module flow chart.

working assignments, enabling participants to experiment with and apply their learning over a one-year period. The philosophy underlying the module sequence is to alternate conceptual with practical modules and technical skill development with interpersonal skill development. Workshop modules are scheduled two to three months apart, depending upon the availability of the participants and the operational requirements of the corporation.

In one instance the curriculum represents a collaborative effort between the company and a university. Participants can receive 15 hours of graduate or undergraduate credit leading to a degree in organization behavior. Instruction is provided by university professors and leading practitioners in the behavioral sciences.

Between workshop modules, work assignments given to the participants create opportunities to practice the skills they have learned. One such assignment provides an experience in introducing an innovation in some area of the company on a trial basis. This gives management an opportunity to observe the effect of using the technology or organization behavior. In addition, participants are examined on a number of articles and texts in the field of organization behavior. A further description of the contents of the modules follows.

Module 1. Assessing historical trends

Before any major change in strategy, policy, structure, or procedure is made, it is important to study the history of the organization and to understand the beginnings, technology resources, structure, and management style. This background is necessary to gain what the Germans term a weltanschauung—a comprehensive view of the organization based on where it has been, where it is now, and where it wants to be in the future. Gaining this view of the organization is analogous to the marketing professional's concern for historical trends that might serve as success predictors of the future.

Therefore, as a first step in the participant's training, he or she is required to conduct an intensive historical study of the organization's goals, technology, structure, products, people, policies, and norms. This assessment then serves as a basis for defining the "culture" of the organization. This module also aims at giving participants a theoretical framework for building analytical skills. The basic concepts of organization behavior are introduced in this module. Participants examine the organizational requirements for undertaking an organizational study.

Module 2. Personal development and planning

Organization members differ widely in their approach to analyzing problems and assessing opportunities, influenced largely by their experience and their know-how in working with behavioral science tools and concepts. In this module an attempt is made to create learning teams that constitute a "live organization." This organization then serves as a focal point for studying organizational dynamics and change.

Participants are divided into small teams that exist through the remaining modules. These teams are responsible for completing tasks assigned by the instructors, evaluating their performance, and contributing in various ways to the total effectiveness of the "organization." Within this organization, participants experience many of the real problems that exist in their work environment: problems of planning, structure, leadership and authority, interdepartmental coordination, team effectiveness, and individual style. An attempt is made to link the learning in the program to parallel situations in the company.

Participants are encouraged to develop an active posture toward their own learning. They become aware of their own learning style, communication behavior, development needs, personal values, and value conflicts. By utilizing a personal journal, participants document their feelings, ideas, observations, and insights about behavior observed in the sessions. This concept is maintained throughout the modules.

Module 3. Diagnosing for planning

Diagnosing a planning system requires an analytical process of identifying and measuring the relevant and valid variables that will make the organization effective and efficient. From this general statement comes the viewpoint that to the extent possible, diagnosis needs to be measurement based, starting with a scientific, quantitative reading of the state of the organization and the direction of movement of organizational change. A rigorous scientific measurement of the way the organization is functioning currently can provide a sound basis for bringing about needed change. Thus, the third module focuses on three major components of diagnosis—data generation, data organization, and data interpretation. Techniques for managing these components are introduced as a means of understanding and applying the basic steps involved in analyzing organizational problems and opportunities.

A significant aspect of the module is the comparison and contrasting of different methods of analysis, including techniques from both the management and behavioral sciences. These methods, together with the skills participants already have, are applied to "real life" problems they are facing in their respective divisions. Participants are also taught that diagnosis is not an end in itself. Rather, it serves the purpose of helping in the total process of planning for improvements in the organization.

Methods for analyzing planning systems, organizational structure, roles and relationships, morale, teamwork, and management style are discussed and practiced in this module. Conducting a proper analysis of these factors following behavioral principles is stressed, since a valid diagnosis increases the probability of applying the right remedies.

Module 4. Planning and the consultation process

The word "consultation" is a general label used to describe the relationship between the adviser and a person or persons in need of counsel. In the context of this program, consultation is simply defined as the process of seeking or giving professional assistance. In a service-oriented economy, the need for professional consulting services has been increasing rapidly since the mid-1960s. Coupled with increased technical specialization, the need for both internal and external consultants in various functional fields will continue to grow.

Consulting economists, planners, financial specialists, operations research experts, management information technologists, personnel advisers, counseling psychologists, and others have become an internal source of assistance to management. Given the rapid increase in the use of consultants and their specific expertise, it is important for managers to understand the process of consultation.

The fourth module is based on the assumption that any major effort to introduce change within a planning system should follow the steps that characterize organization behavior consultation. These steps include such actions as (1) establishing a working relationship with management, (2) planning the data collection methods and expected outcomes of the project, and (3) establishing criteria to evaluate the progress of the effort. Participants are exposed to the psychological dynamics that affect interpersonal relationships.

An integral part of this module is the designing of a plan to assist the management of a specific department to identify, analyze, and resolve an operating or relationship problem. The design of the module allows participants to apply the skills they are learning to real situations. The opportunity to use team, peer, and professional resources during this module enables each member to give and receive feedback in both the role of expert and that of collaborator.

Module 5. Theory and methods for introducing change

To introduce change into an organization, it is necessary to alter the basic processes of information flow, data gathering, decision making, and communication. Change can be introduced in a variety of ways. It can be mandated to lower organizational levels by senior management. It can come about as a result of the organizational unit doing something to itself. Or it can occur through joint collaboration that takes place between consultant and managers.

In Module 5, participants are taught how to initiate activities designed to improve the functioning of their own departments and are advised on how to consult with managers outside their work unit. The theory and practice of introducing change are based on four major themes related to the individual functioning as a consultant: (1) personal values; (2) assumptions about man, organizations, and interpersonal relations; (3) goals for himself, for the organization, and for its members; (4) and a series of analytical methods that serve as the means for implementing these values, assumptions, and goals.

During the course of this module, participants are provided with an opportunity to simulate the implementation of a structural reorganization, an attitude survey, a work-planning system, and other organizational changes. By the end of this module, participants are expected to be able to identify the criteria for designing a change strategy, begin a change effort, manage the project, and evaluate the results.

Module 6. Project review and skills clinic

During the course of this training program, participants have the responsibility of identifying and developing an organizational problem or opportunity for analysis in one of six topical areas: strategic or operational planning, organizational structure, staff–line roles, teamwork, morale, or management effectiveness. Participants are required to outline the purpose, scope, and methodology of their projects, which have been a part of their practices since the first module. These presentations are then followed by discussion and critique, with the staff serving as facilitators and as resources for learning.

An equal portion of the participant's time is spent on experimental exercises designed to develop practical evaluation skills. Members of the learning teams outline and discuss the issues, strategies, and alternative techniques of project evaluation that will be useful for further interventions. Particular emphasis is given to the methods they intend to use to analyze the problem area, their implementation strategy, and their evaluation criteria.

Working with the instructors, participants are encouraged to design a personal development plan based on their background, experience, interest, and current level of interpersonal and technical competency. To further their development they select at least one major topical area (such as structural reorganization, job design, or work-flow analysis) in which to get more training after this module is completed.

After completing the curriculum, participants are equipped to use behavioral techniques for planning purposes. Often they start by introducing organization behavior concepts to other managers in their work area, "marketing" the idea of using the technology of the discipline for planning or solving operating and interpersonal problems. Their proximity to the operating end of the business offers an opportunity to reinforce the values and assumptions of organization behavior continually through educational and demonstration efforts.

When they have finished the training program, individuals should be able to fill at least one of the following roles:

Assist in the analysis of the planning process
Help create an intent to change (if change is needed)
Help translate this intent into action
Help stabilize the change and prevent discontinuance

To fill one or more of these roles, participants selected for the program must first be viewed as credible within the organization. Thus selection criteria should be established to ensure that those selected to attend will have the qualities that are representative of the company in terms of values, past experience, concern, and character. The criteria include:

Administrative skills
Emotional stabililty
Interpersonal skills
Personal leadership skills
Potential for personal development
Problem-analysis skills
Technical competence
Work-oriented motivation

In addition, each participant should be recommended by his or her respective line or staff divisions. Position level is often less important in the selection process than perceived success. Preferably a wide variety of position levels and business functions should be represented.

The strategy of training internal personnel, who then use organization behavior approaches on a trial basis for introducing changes in the planning process that can be observed and evaluated before they are institutionalized, meets an important requirement for introducing change: It demonstrates the advantage of change on a limited basis in situations where users can observe its impact. Transferring the skills and technology from professional planners to line managers removes the mystique that is often associated with planning and goes a long way toward making change reasonably easy to understand.

Implications

The concept of creating an organizationwide understanding of organization behavior principles and practices associated with planning is in itself a change effort. What can be gained from this effort?

In the future, organizations will have to become more involved in the quality of working life for employees. In November 1975, President Gerald Ford signed into law a bill establishing the National Center for Productivity and the Quality of Working Life. This action was precipitated by the evolution of issues and concerns related to the quality of working life over the past 25 years. Events such as this will require managers to move toward more participative organizational practices. The approach outlined here reflects an attempt to provide managers with the resources that permit them to respond appropriately to these trends.

A network of internal personnel training in behavioral technology provides a mechanism for increasing an organization's capacity for upward, downward, horizontal, and diagonal communication. Personnel trained in this program can *provide management* with:

An effective and efficient information retrieval and dissemination capability for the formation and implementation of plans.

Immediate response to requests for clarification or continuation of information about the plans.

Information on the "pulse" of the organization.

An effective link between corporate division and site locations for planning, goal-setting, and other work-flow requirements.

Network personnel can also be available to help managers implement new program policies. A common complaint heard among managers is that they are often expected to implement new programs or alter existing systems with little or no assistance. Programs are often introduced into their operations—new maintenance systems, purchasing procedures, performance review requirements, Equal Employment Opportunity (EEO) guidelines—that ultimately produce confusion and mixed results.

Since many managers believe that their job is to "manage the business, not new programs," many changes can neither be consolidated nor evaluated. Using this approach makes personnel available to help managers implement new programs and policies. The availability of personnel trained to use the technology of organization behavior in marketing, manufacturing, technical, and other functions provides management with multiple resources for introducing change as well as the organization environment that must accommodate these interventions.

The network also provides personal development opportunities for high-potential personnel and special organizational recognition for long-term employees. This factor alone makes the program comparatively advantageous.

Another advantage is that it provides a resource to management at the level of need in the hierarchy instead of concentrating the technology of planning in a small corporate staff. The network actually functions as a pyramiding device to market corporate objectives more quickly and more broadly than could be done even by a large corporate staff.

Last, the concept of a consulting network creates widespread attention and understanding of the nature, scope, and purpose of organization behavior. In attempting to develop organization behavior as a viable discipline, it is important for line management to understand the theory and to monitor the results of consulting efforts. Because so many trends and fads in the behavioral sciences have been applied to the business world over the past twenty or thirty years, managers are often perplexed by the technical terminology (intervention, role analysis, team building, conflict resolution, unfreezing, change agent, and so on). With an effective marketing strategy, the potential exists to create a corporatewide semantic awareness and, perhaps even more important, to delimit and define organization behavior concepts further within the framework of ongoing business practices.

Organization behavior constitutes a method for approaching the broad problem of introducing change and has proved effective in many pragmatic applications. To prevent the discipline from being viewed as a passing fad or as a program with only temporary quality, practitioners must discover new ways to market its benefits. If our aim is to improve the organization's internal resource capability to meet the inevitable change of the future, we must find the proper mechanism to effectuate a transfer of behavior technology from staff functions to line operations. An effective marketing strategy is one approach to this end.

Summary

Managing in today's environment requires the ability both to maintain the profitability of the business and to change the business environment itself. Historically, organizations have selected and developed managers who have the ability to maintain the business by managing the flow of products and services at a profit. Since the maintenance aspect of the management function requires highly practical approaches to problem solving, managers are often selected on the basis of their capacity to conform, their desire for predictability, and their ability to control.

The process of change, then, is often left to outside consultants, senior management, staff specialists, or occasionally a maverick manager. And with good reason. Although operating managers may yearn for a more innovative role, the maintenance requirements of their job trap them by consuming their time, narrowing their view of the organization, and rewarding them for meeting profit-and-loss objectives.

Yet the need to bring about change, to tap a wide range of human resources at all levels in the hierarchy, is critical as organizations are confronted with emerging technologies, rising costs, and the need for increased organizational efficiency. Executive management cannot afford the luxury of waiting for changes to occur or for innovators to emerge. Both must be sought out. People and ideas that are diverse, uncertain, dynamic, and unprogrammed must become a part of the organization's planning and decision-making process. However, not unlike the maintenance manager, these people and their ideas need to be managed.

II

Organizing for Increased Profitability

The degree to which a corporation's potential for excellence is realized depends upon management's ability to recognize operating deficiencies and to take remedial action. Rapid market growth, cyclical ups and downs of the business, or day-to-day problems often tend to obscure operational shortcomings. Problems related to the workings of many departments may go unnoticed for long periods of time—until disruption affects the bottom line. For example, a shortage of supplies, external controls, economic slowdowns, or dramatic declines in employee productivity may provide unwelcome assistance in exposing unproductive or loosely managed functional areas. Unfortunately, such unwelcome assistance usually uncovers a crisis rather than a manageable problem, leaving many a discredited executive in its wake.

For an organization to realize its full performance potential, it must have the capability of identifying improvement opportunities regularly and the wherewithal to develop management action plans to bring about needed changes. Traditional analytical techniques are often applied to line and staff operations as well as to product or market performance. Evaluations of line operations generally focus on major performance problems as they may precede acquisition or divestiture decisions. Such studies usually assess the viability or the overall organizational structure of a specific operation. Staff effectiveness studies typically focus on the scope of efforts or cost of services and often result in a reorientation of objectives, organizational restructuring, or staff resizing. Performance audits of selected products or markets are designed to assist management in developing strategies to increase cash or profit contributions through improved utilization of assets.

There are, however, two major problems associated with most attempts to gain increased profits through reorganization. The first problem is that many companies attempt to reorganize their operations by using conventional approaches to analyze and design their structure(s). The second problem is that management pays little attention to the critical issues associated with implementing organizational change. Both problems are potentially very costly. In this section we shall examine them and propose alternative approaches for analyzing organizational structure and implementing a change effort.

5

Approaches to analyzing structure

THE WAY in which people's jobs and responsibilities are integrated in a company has a significant effect on the efficiency with which it operates. Although no scientific studies (known to the author) have demonstrated causal relationships between organizational structure and productivity, it is a well-accepted fact that improperly designed structures can lead to major business problems. Still, in many companies, managers seem to take less interest in the organization's structure than in other aspects of their jobs.

Most managers are fully aware of the concept of pyramiding people in a structure and are conscious of the traditional terminology of span of control and line and staff distinctions. However, they are uneasy with the thought of analyzing the effectiveness or appropriateness of their existing structure. Thus, the tendency of many managers is to rely on conventional approaches for analyzing and designing structure.

Conventional Approaches

There may be any number of reasons for this uneasiness in dealing with questions related to structure, but one seems apparent: Few managers are ever exposed to any methodical approaches for analyzing and designing structure. When faced with the question of how to organize, management often turns to personnel departments, which are asked to "draw up an organization chart," or to management consulting firms, which are asked to study the business and recommend an appropriate structure.

In most companies, the personnel function is no more equipped to conduct the proper analysis necessary for an effective design than the manager requesting the assistance is. More characteristically, the company's senior executive will rely on a management consulting firm to conduct the study and formulate organizational recommendations. Most principals employed by management consulting firms to conduct this kind of work are schooled in business and finance rather than the behavioral disciplines. The approaches used, therefore, and the recommendations offered often ignore some very important organization behavior issues related to such factors as the availability of personnel, selection and placement of key personnel, decision-making processes, management style, and management development.

Outside assistance is often an invaluable resource for studies related to organizational structure. On the other hand, management consultants often ignore, or pass over lightly, efforts within the organization that are directed at long-term change and development in favor of examining only financial objectives and overhead costs. One company, for example, was advised by a management consulting firm to cut back its college recruiting programs substantially as part of a cost reduction objective, only to find two years later that it faced serious shortages of engineers, scientists, and financial and employee relations personnel. The cost of recovering from these shortages proved to be five times greater than the original "savings."

In the past, it was convenient to analyze organizational structure with simple yardsticks such as span of control, ratio of managers to supervisors to direct labor, work unit size, product line, staff and line distinctions, or the shape of the company's hierarchy.

Today, these categories are no longer sufficient for examining or designing structures that are responsive to the emerging needs and decision-making processes characteristic of modern business. The increase in technology, the higher level of worker competencies, the intricacies of planning (referred to in earlier chapters), and the changes in employee expectations (discussed in later chapters), to name but a few of the recent changes in doing business, have created a need for a more careful identification of the resource needs and structural relationships arising de facto from business strategy and policy, task requirements, business objectives, and individual expertise and initiative.

Yet in spite of these changes, many companies continue to rely on tradition and outdated approaches for analyzing and changing organizational structures and roles that are not responsive to emerging information needs and decision-making processes. Realigning a division or department for the sole purpose of reducing a manager's span of reporting relationships usually creates interface problems, information blockage, decision bottlenecks, morale problems, and other costly problems. Designing "logical" reporting relationships by drawing up organization charts and setting position levels that balance the ratio of superiors to subordinates may be in conflict with the company's strategy of emphasizing one product or program over another.

Conveniently organizing by product line may impede a company's effort to expand its market share through forward or backward integration. Organizing around basic staff and line distinctions may encourage parochial thinking or result in the creation of sophisticated systems by staff people that are neither understood nor used by line personnel. Designing a highly pyramidical or a flat structure may not be consistent with the company's preferred management style or with the available management resources.

In sum, the conventional approaches used to analyze and design organizational structures are no longer relevant. The task of structuring an organization should not be left entirely up to either the personnel department or outside consulting firms. More than ever, managers must be brought into the process of analyzing their own departments as well as the departments with whom they must interface. The study of organization breaches departmental boundaries. The launching of a new product, for example, must be analyzed by means of a communications network covering all necessary departmental interfaces, including research and development, purchasing, advertising, production, and others. Also adding new businesses or expanding existing ones necessitates crossing departmental lines for such tasks as designing the construction of a new production facility, selecting managers to supervise, or training salesmen to market the products. Ignoring these factors can increase rather than decrease the cost of doing business.

Alternative Approaches

Most experts will agree that conventional approaches to analyzing structure are no longer relevant, but there appears to be an absence of alternative approaches. The findings and observations related to the question of what organizational factors affect or are affected by structure have led to many lengthy, often highly theoretical, writings. The theories and models resulting from these deliberations are far too numerous to discuss here. However, the conclusions that have emerged from the many disciplines that concern themselves with the study of organizational structure generally fall into two major areas: those that focus on the analysis of departments or small work units and those that focus on the analysis of the total organization.

Factors Related to Departmental Structure

Organizational research in the behavioral sciences (particularly in the field of psychology) has typically focused on individual and small-group behavior as it pertains to questions of structure. The conclusions drawn from this field of study are usually applied to departments or small divisions, but only rarely to total company structure. Studies examining such variables as size, span of control, number of hierarchical levels, authority structures, communication processes, status and prestige, and psychological distance between managers and subordinates are abundant in behavioral science literature.

In synthesizing a large number of organizational structure studies conducted over a period of 25 years, Lawrence R. James and Allan C. Jones concluded that there are seven major factors (or relevant variables) that should be taken into consideration in any examination of organizational structure:*

1. Total organization size.
2. Centralization/decentralization of decision making and authority.
3. Configuration including communication structures, number of levels in the hierarchy, span of control, and differentiation of work groups.
4. Formalization of procedures, roles, status, prestige, emphasis on going through channels, and extent of written communications.
5. Specialization or division of labor according to functional and task specialization and line and staff hierarchies.
6. Standardization of procedures and tasks.
7. Interdependence of organizational tasks and autonomy with respect to intraorganizational functions.

These factors are useful in that, when taken together, they incorporate a number of important observable and measurable organizational conditions that can directly affect the state of the busi-

* "Organizational Structure: A Review of Structural Dimensions and Their Conceptual Relationships with Individual Attitudes and Behavior," *Organizational Behavior and Human Performance,* vol. 16, 1976.

ness. They have further utility when used as a frame of reference for analyzing the condition of a department or small organizational unit before any attempts are made to redesign or realign the structure.

Most researchers and practitioners would agree that these dimensions are applicable to the study of organizational structure, but the research on individual and small-group behavior has not yet produced a systematic procedure that can be used to analyze and design structures above an immediate work group. The research on how people behave in an organization is generally void of any knowledge on how to assess the characteristics of the business or how to design a hierarchy that conforms to the strategic plans of the organization. Furthermore, the task of integrating these factors into a meaningful, usable approach to organizing has been left to practitioners who, because of the conceptual nature of these studies, often disregard important findings and implications in favor of the more conventional methods of analyzing and designing structure.

Analyzing such factors as size, procedures, or task specialization is helpful in determining the health of the organization and the relative effectiveness of communications, work flow, and decision making. By using James' and Jones's seven factors as major criteria and then developing questions related to these factors, practitioners can analyze the strengths and weaknesses of departments or small work units.

This type of analytical work does not account for conditions outside the work unit that may have an influence on the effectiveness of the structure. Thus it is useful in correcting structural differences only on a microorganizational level. Yet it can provide an invaluable assessment of several organizational processes that ultimately will affect productivity to some extent. The identification of decision-making efficiency, communication effectiveness, role expectancies, accountability issues, and so forth is an essential first step toward the consideration of structural reorganization.

Factors Related to Total Company Structure

In recent years, a number of scholars in the sociology, political science, and management science disciplines have begun investigations that focus on the match between the formal structure of an organization and its environment. In the most general sense, their perspective is that organizational structure is heavily dependent on such factors as the company's markets, its technology, and the culture within which it exists. Since these factors vary widely, it is generally reasoned that organizational structures will vary accordingly. This view is represented in two major theories: the systems theory and the contingency theory.

Systems theory

The word "system" as used in this context refers to a set of interdependent, interacting elements that, when added together, form an organized unit. When functioning properly, this unit is capable of producing output greater than the output of the separate elements if they functioned independently. A manufacturing organization, for example, can be called a system in that it comprises a number of separate units: marketing, engineering, finance, and research and development. Functioning separately, these units are of little value. Taken as a whole, they constitute a system that designs, manufactures, and markets products.

Applying systems theory to the analysis of organizational structure is difficult. Most systems theorists discuss organizational structure in general terms by calling attention to the relationship among social, psychological, economic, and technical forces at work in the environment and to the effects these forces have on the various subsystems in the organization. Figure 7 represents an organization viewed as a system.

The outside square represents the external environment that must be analyzed before the strategy is developed. The strategy

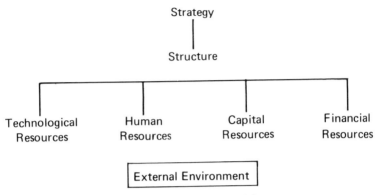

Figure 7. Systems theory organizational model.

provides the target for the organization's efforts and serves as the focal point for designing the structure. The structure serves as an integrating mechanism for the organization's resources. It defines relationships within the system, including reporting relationships, formal procedures, policies, decision authority, and coordination of work flow.

The technological resources consist of the procedures, methods, and technical knowledge unique to the organization. Human resources are the skills and abilities of organization members, leadership style and philosophy, and formal and informal communications networks. Capital resources include the organization's physical assets, properties, machines, and other economic goods used in production. Financial resources are the organization's capacity to raise and expand the corporation's revenue.

The systems approach contributes to our understanding of what organizational factors to study; it provides a useful frame of reference for recognizing the relationship between structure and the other forces at work inside and outside the organization. Clearly demonstrating that these relationships exist, the theory still falls short of explaining how these forces interact and fails to demonstrate precise implications for analyzing or designing structures at a macroorganizational level.

Contingency theory

Like the systems theory, the contingency theory recognizes the importance of the interrelationship between the organization and its environment. Unlike systems theory, contingency theory has gone beyond a description of these relationships and has indicated the kinds of structure that may be appropriate for different kinds of organizational conditions.

A study conducted by Joan Woodward in 1958 in 100 manufacturing firms in England is often cited as one of the pioneering efforts that led to the formation of contingency theory. Her original intent was to determine if selected principles of management were observed in the companies she studied. Her most important discovery was that differences in technology (measured on a scale ranging from custom production to mass production to continuous-process production) accounted for differences in organizational structure. She discovered, for example, that the average number of employees controlled by first-line supervisors varied from 25 in custom production to 50 in mass production to 11 in continuous-process production.

After this study, a number of scholars began examining other variables that have a major impact on organizational structure, such as size, environmental factors, market potential, and technology. Paul Lawrence and Jay Lorsch, two professors at the Harvard Business School, have advanced the contingency theory through an organizational model that focuses on the two major dimensions that they call integration and differentiation.*

The integration–differentiation model suggests that it is possible for a single divisionalized company to have multiple organizational structures. The communication configurations necessary for decision making and information transfers could vary from one division to another. The variation would depend on (1) the degree to which the division must communicate with other operations or

* *Developing Organizations: Diagnosis and Action.* Reading, Mass.: Addison-Wesley, 1969.

functions to accomplish its mission (integration) and (2) the degree to which its mission differs from the mission of other operations or functions in terms of both product and service (differentiation). This concept emphasizes the view that large formal organizations must be thought of in terms of smaller, interrelated suborganizations. The integration–differentiation model, instead of providing a universal prescription of one best way to organize, provides a framework for identifying the operational requirements each suborganization must satisfy in order to perform effectively.

To understand the operating requirements of an organization, it is necessary to look at how much differentiation exists among various organizational units. For example, if the suborganizations in the company (such as the market, scientific know-how, techno-economic, and manufacturing factors) are fairly homogeneous in their degree of specialization, the units will need to be fairly similar in formal organizational and management practices. If they have quite different degrees of specialization, the units will need to be more differentiated.

The integration dimension of the model requires an identification of the operating divisions or functions that are required to work together as well as a definition of the degree to which they are interdependent. Where operating groups, because of their particular tasks, are highly differentiated, it is more difficult to achieve integration among them. As a result, when groups in an organization need to be highly differentiated but also require a high degree of integration, the organization needs to develop more complicated integrating mechanisms. The basic organizational mechanism for achieving integration is, of course, the management hierarchy.

In organizations with low differentiation, basic traditional structures are sufficient. However, organizations that require a high degree of both differentiation and integration must develop supplemental integrating devices, such as individual coordinators, cross-unit teams, and even whole departments whose basic contribution is to achieve integration among other organizational groups or units. By using this model, then, we can understand not only the pattern of integration required to deal effectively with a particular environment, but also the formal structural devices needed to achieve this pattern.

Other researchers have examined specific relationships between organizational technology and structure. Charles Perrow, a sociologist, has suggested, for example, that organizations employing "engineering technology" tend to be centralized but flexible, whereas those employing "craft technology" (when the work involved is fairly uniform) tend to be decentralized.*

Contingency theory has contributed significantly to our understanding of how the organization's technology and integration processes relate to the way in which the organization as a whole should be structured. The concepts of scholars like Woodward, Lawrence and Lorsch, and Perrow have helped shape contemporary organizational research. Most contemporary approaches to examining overall company structure borrow heavily from contingency theory in shaping the concepts used to analyze and design organizational structures.

The systems and contingency theories have taught us that organizational structure cannot be viewed in isolation from other external and internal organizational factors. The specialized nature of the organizational technology must be considered. The need to integrate the company's total resource base must also be considered. The relationship between discrete business functions must be analyzed thoroughly. The market potential of the company's products must be assessed.

Although these two theories have identified some of the factors that must be considered when analyzing organizational structure, they have omitted the two most important factors—company strategy and management resources. These two must be assessed before any decision on how to organize can be made. In Chapter 6

---

* "A Framework for the Comparative Analysis of Organizations," *American Sociological Review,* vol. 32, 1967.

I attempt to integrate them into a model that can be used to analyze structure. Before turning to the question of how to analyze organizational structure, let's list the factors that must be analyzed prior to designing the structure.

Total size of the organization
Effectiveness of communication
Efficiency of decision making
Work-flow efficiency
Formal organizational policies
Work procedures
Type of business, such as high technology, heavy
    manufacturing, or retail
Preferred management style
Depth of management and technical resources
Degree of integration among business functions
Degree of differentiation among business functions
Interdependence of organizational tasks
Number of levels in the hierarchy
Spans of management control
Company strategy
Operating business objectives

Summary

The task of analyzing organizational factors is often far beyond the reach of management. The trends toward increased company size, growing specialization of experts comprising the management team, centralization of information and planning, and a changing attitude by the workforce (discussed in Chapter 9) cannot be accommodated easily within most traditional organizational structures. Simple distinctions between line and staff work are no longer apparent. Delegating the task of analyzing these factors to untrained staff employees is no longer enough to respond to the demands of the business. Managers often must work on project teams, task forces, and other integrating work units to analyze structural problems. How to organize is an important decision that cannot be left in the hands of a third party.

In the chapter that follows, I attempt to fit the 16 factors just cited into a model that can be used by management as a guide for analyzing organizational structure. The process of analyzing and designing structure usually requires professional assistance, but a reading of this chapter will help management to understand how organizational studies should be conducted and provide a frame of reference for assessing the quality and logic of the analytical work that precedes the design of a structure.

6

How to analyze structure

ANY DISCUSSION on how to structure an organization should begin with the assumption that there are no best ways to organize. The process of analyzing and designing structure is both an art and a science—the analysis more a science, the design more an art. The approach to analyzing organizational structure that I am advocating can be applied to the overall structure of the organization (the superstructure) or to the subunits within the organization (the infrastructures).

Using the findings from scholars who have contributed to our understanding of both micro and macro issues related to organizational structure, my own experience, and the experience of my colleagues in analyzing and designing structures in a variety of multinational business organizations, I have identified five basic elements that need to be analyzed in any structural study. They are the company's strategic business plan, technology, policies, communication patterns, and management resources.

Strategic Business Plan

As discussed in earlier chapters, the effective employment of company resources requires the development and implementation of a definite strategy. The strategy must designate the business areas selected for emphasis and allocate resources accordingly. The planning of strategy for each business unit determines the full range of potential for existing business lines. Regardless of shifts in direction required by external or internal conditions, there are fundamental guidelines in most company strategies that will not change frequently. These generally include statements of rationale for allocating resources, dealing with factors such as investment criteria, priorities for growth, technological advances, and acquisition, divestment, and diversification opportunities. In short, the company's strategic direction usually identifies a profile for each of its business units. Any analysis or design of structure should be guided by the specific elements of this profile.

Consider, for example, one company's statement of strategic intent to have one of its major product lines grow through new-product development. An analysis of the structure revealed that no jobs were designated as new-product-development jobs. Furthermore, a review of the company's budget showed that no money was budgeted for new-product development. Interviews with key management personnel revealed that no one felt accountable for developing new products. In short, the company's organizational structure was not designed to support the strategic plan of the organization.

In another instance, a company developed a five-year plan to diversify its business by acquiring companies that were suppliers of parts used to assemble large conveyor systems. During the first three years of this planning cycle, no acquisitions were made and only two prospective candidates had been reviewed by the company's top management. An examination of the organization clearly demonstrated a lack of functional responsibility and accountability for identifying and analyzing acquisition opportunities. The company did not succeed in attaining its strategic objectives until a staff department was formed and chartered with acquisition responsibility.

The question of how to organize must begin, therefore, with a thorough understanding of the strategy for each business unit. Just

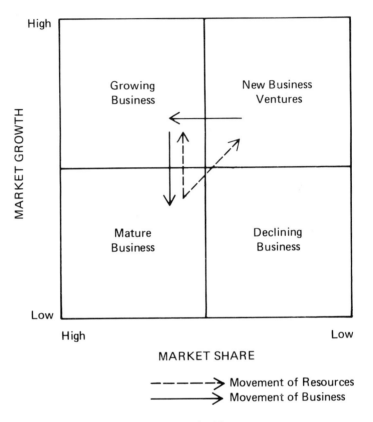

Figure 8. Movement of resources and of business.

as the movement of resources must follow the movement of business (see Figure 8), the structural alignment of people must be consistent with the aims of the business. An effective analysis of the strategy should yield answers to the following questions.

- What elements of the company's strategic plan are not being served by the current organizational structure?

- What broad business opportunities has the company identified for development? Are there statements with respect to:

Timing (near term versus long term)?
Technological versus marketing?
Impact on company size?
Impact on company business mix?

- Are there any business operating needs that need to be served at a corporate level such as:
Market or product research?
Technical research and development?
Financial services?
Human resource planning?

- Are there strategic intents to acquire? If so, will the acquisitions fit into existing business units or will they become separate business entities?

- Are there strategic intents to divest? If so, how much of the company's business will be affected? How many and what types of people will be involved?

- Are there strategic indicators that characterize the company's operations as:
Growing businesses?
Mature businesses?
New businesses?
Declining businesses?

- Does the company's strategy call for:
The maintenance of market viability in existing markets?
An increase in market share in existing markets with existing products?
An increase in market share in existing markets with new products?
Penetrating new markets with existing products or with new products?

- Does the company's strategy identify any major projects that are designed to reduce costs or improve production?

- Are there any strategic statements that suggest possible synergies among operating business units?

Structure must be linked to strategy. The design of new jobs and the creation of new departments should be the result of a strategic plan that calls out their need. Also, the elimination of a job or a department should be the result of a strategic plan that excludes their need as part of a shift in direction or as part of a cost reduction effort. Determining the size of a department and the depth of management and technical resources can be done only with a clear understanding of how and where management intends to allocate its resources in support of its business plan.

Technology

As organizations grow in size and scope, they generally need both higher technical specialization and more sophisticated control systems. Companies that have discrete technologies or highly specialized products may need several different kinds of organizational structures to support their business strategies and day-to-day operating requirements.

The principles of contingency theory can be used to assess the type of technology present in the organization as a whole or in its subsystems. For example, in a large divisionalized company, there may be varying degrees of technological specialization, ranging from subsystems that are highly specialized (such as research and development) to subsystems with low specialization (such as routine mass production areas). Although there may be no established standards to quantify the degrees of technological differentiation without an organization, a review of the tasks performed and an analysis of the kinds of specialized skills needed to perform these tasks can serve as an analytical base for making judgments.

To conduct the proper analysis, it is helpful to look at the relationship between technological specialization and various types of organizational structure. In Figure 9 I have identified four different forms of organizational structure. Each form is a variation of the preceding one, beginning with a basic line–staff organization,

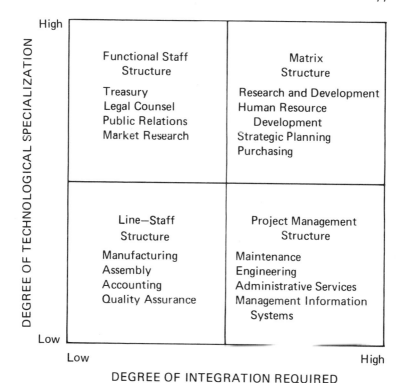

Figure 9. Technology and organizational form.

which is most applicable in organizing business units that are not highly specialized technologically. The matrix structure is best used when business units are highly specialized technologically and are interdependent.

An effective analysis of the organization's technology should answer these questions:

- To what degree is the company's technology (or technologies) specialized?
- Is a high degree of integration required among the company's varying technologies?

- Has the company's technological base expanded to the point where staff support services are required? If so, should these services remain with line operations (low specialization) or become a separate staff department (high specialization)?
- Does the company intend to maintain, expand, or narrow its technological base?

An effective analysis of a company's structure must include an assessment of technology. Organizational form is related to technological integration and specialization requirements as follows.

The *line–staff* organization is most appropriate when roles, duties, and responsibilities are well defined, and not much integration with other organizational units is required. The line–staff organization is easy to manage in terms of automation and time-and-motion methods, and yields fairly predictable output or efficiency ratings. Emphasis is on capital resources utilization.

The *functional staff* organization is most appropriate when roles, duties, and responsibilities are not quite as well defined and little integration with other organizational units is required. This form of organization fits situations in which the specialization required cannot be managed easily through the process of automation, time-and-motion methods, or other methods that yield fairly predictable output or efficiency ratings. Emphasis is on technology or expertise utilization.

The *project management* form of organization is most appropriate when roles, duties, and responsibilities are somewhat defined and when integration with other organizational units is extremely desirable and required. This approach to organizational structuring fits situations in which specialization is easy to manage in terms of automation, time-and-motion methods, or other methods that yield fairly predictable output or efficiency ratings. Emphasis is on workforce utilization.

The *matrix* form of organization is most appropriate when roles, duties, and responsibilities overlap somewhat and integration with other organizational units is not only required, but essential to successful goal attainment. This approach fits situations in which specialization is not easy to manage in terms of automation, time-and-motion studies, or other methods that yield fairly predictable output or efficiency ratings. Emphasis is on multiple use of resources.

Assessing the specialization and integration requirements of each major organizational unit is an important second step in analyzing structure. This step is especially necessary when companies undertake a reorganization of their total operation. The results of this form of analysis should prevent management from making the costly mistake of viewing all its businesses within the same organizational framework. Although a matrix structure may be well suited to a business or department with high specialization and integration needs, it is ill suited to a business or department that has technology characterized by low specialization and integration needs.

Policy

In most companies certain management controls are established at the corporate level to assure that individual organizational units provide common contributions. To communicate and enforce these controls, authority is centralized, because in certain instances decentralized decision making can lead to local decisions that are counterproductive to desired or required company objectives. Policies are the means for defining these needs and constitute a method for identifying and communicating those areas in which decision making will be centralized. Policy formulation is the vehicle by which management assures the proper balance between central direction and local decision making.

Policies may include directions for managers to implement policy objectives, conditions for central decision making, conditions for local decision making with reports to a central point, or conditions for local decision making in adherence to policy. Policies issued by the company's top management generally cover a limited number of areas of conduct or procedure. Policies at lower levels in the organization usually deal with subjects relating to the functional responsibilities of specific departments. Often, they are designed to guide or direct the procedures, activities, or decisions of managers. Policies that guide staff functions may take the form of stated internal administrative procedures outlining the flow of communication that should occur before and after decision making. The design of an organizational structure should be closely aligned to policy. Decisions to centralize or decentralize will be affected by policy statements. Establishing an effective structure requires clear statements of policy that delineate reservations of authority and document mandatory, consistent courses of action.

In analyzing structure, the following policy questions should be addressed:

- Does (do) the organizational unit(s) under study have policies that address issues related to:
  Optimization of cost?
  Standards of performance?
  Assessment of responsibilities?
- If policies exist, do they call for central or local decision making?
- Have certain responsibilities and objectives been established at the corporate level to ensure that individual organizational units provide common contributions?
- Has authority been reserved in some areas because decentralized decision making could lead to local decisions that are counterproductive to desired or required company objectives?
- Are existing policies only reservations of authority or do they include directions for managers throughout the company designed to implement policy objectives?

Most organizations have two basic kinds of policies. The broadest form of policy is the policy directive. It is issued by the company's top management and covers a limited number of areas of conduct or procedure. Directive policies deal with issues of major significance to the company's well-being and require mandatory and consistent adherence, special emphasis, and a high level of attention and monitoring. Top management reserves the authority to direct decisions in areas affected by these policies.

The second kind of policy is the functional policy. It deals with subjects related to the decision-making responsibilities of the company's business units. The functional policy is intended to guide or direct procedures, activities, or decisions of managers and other employees throughout the company. For example, policies related to the purchase of materials, the pricing of products, hiring practices, and the monitoring and reporting of financial results often delineate the functional areas (such as purchasing, marketing, personnel, and finance) responsible for establishing and enforcing policy adherence.

The design of an organizational structure, the determination of position titles, and job content should be guided by functional policy statements. A careful analysis of functional policy should precede any attempt to design a structure. When there are no functional policies or when revisions are needed, care should be taken to form functional policies that clearly establish guidelines for decision making, set procedures, and define broad areas of responsibility.

Statements of internal administrative procedure should not be confused with functional policy statements. Internal administrative procedures are straightforward statements of routine procedure that apply only to specific work units. These procedures usually require no approvals beyond that of the issuing work unit head. Statements of internal administrative procedures should state that they apply only to the staff (including "resident personnel") of the issuing work unit and not to other employees of the company.

Table 3. Comparisons of policies and procedures.

Policies	Issued	Approved	Affects
Directive policies	Top management	Top management	All company employees
Functional policies	Functional head	Top management's functional head	Applicable functional areas of an organizational unit in the company
Internal administrative procedures	Work unit head	Functional head Work unit head	Issuing work unit

Internal administrative procedures should not be used as the basis for designing an organizational structure. They are of value in clarifying responsibilities and work activities once a structure has been established. In analyzing organizational policies, it is essential to separate directive and functional policies that guide structural decisions from internal administrative procedures that should be put in place once a structure has been established. Table 3 compares the two forms of policy with administrative procedures on the basis of who issues, approves, and is affected by the statements.

Communications

Fundamentally there are two important occasions for communication in organization. The first is when decisions must be made. The search for information in the form of reports, discussion, and other types of communication necessary before, during, and after decision making creates a flow of communication in vertical, lateral, and horizontal directions. The second is when attempts are made to modify the behavior of people in the organization through policy, directives, demands, or persuasion. The structure of the organization must be designed to facilitate both decision making and communication about decisions.

The question of how to structure an organization is really a question of how to arrange the configuration of communication patterns between individuals, between individuals and groups, and between groups and other groups. To illustrate this concept, it might be helpful to think of the relationship between large operating divisions of a company and the whole corporation in terms of a network of communications. A communications network consists of decision centers that seek, receive, transmit, subdivide, classify, store, select, recall, and recombine information. The network is formed by the arrangement of these decision centers into an organizational structure.

The arrangement of decision centers begins with an analysis of the discrete business functions that must be performed on a regular basis in order to produce products and services for the market. This can be accomplished by building a grid like the one in Figure 10. In this example, the major decisions that must be made are indicated in the left column. The functional areas needed to gather, synthesize, evaluate, and communicate information pertaining to these decisions are indicated across the top of the grid. *A* indicates the functional area that has the final authority to make the decision; *C* is used to designate those functional areas that must be consulted before a final decision is made.

An effective analysis of structure should address questions related to the perceived effectiveness of communications within the organization. Questions such as the following can be used as guidelines for assessing the quality of communication flow.

• To what extent is information about important decisions shared within specific work units?

Decisions Related to	Marketing	Manufacturing	Planning and Development	Employee Relations	Controller
New product development	C	C	A		
Pricing	A	C			C
Purchasing		A			C
Market expansion	A	C	C		
Inventory levels	C	A			C
Production scheduling	C	A			
Advertising	A				
Operating budgets	C	C	C	C	A
Wage and salary guidelines	C	C	C	C	A

A = Final authority to make the decision.
C = Areas that must be consulted before final decision is made.

Figure 10. Making decisions with the help of a grid.

- To what extent are people informed of changes that affect their work?
- How clearly are company aims and plans understood within the structure?
- How adequate is the amount of information shared among departments?
- Is decision making highly centralized?
- How willing is the company to discuss policies, plans, and actions that affect work productivity?
- How well do employees understand their work assignments?
- Do employees have a clear idea of what is expected from them?

The answers to these questions can help determine the nature, extent, and variability of communication demands that exist within the current structure. Identifying the decision centers and assessing the communication flow can serve as a valuable aid in closing the gap between conditions currently obtainable and the conditions that should prevail. The process of identifying the decision centers and information channels for each operation in the system will help determine the type of organizational structure that will best accommodate the organization's strategy, technology, and policies.

Management Resources

Perhaps the most neglected factor considered in most organizational studies is the quantity and quality of the company's management resources. Yet of all the factors involved in the design of a structure, the depth and breadth of management capability to organize and direct the work of the corporation's human resource is the most vital.

Without an adequate inventory of the skills, knowledge, experience, and other qualifications available within the organization, a great deal of time and money can be wasted by designing an organizational structure that cannot function properly with the type of managers available. The question of managerial span of control, for example, usually relates more to the skill of the manager than to other organizational factors. Establishing dual reporting relationships by matrixing the structure may or may not facilitate communications and decision making, depending once again on managerial capacity to coordinate and manage multiple communication flow. Where positions are highly differentiated and highly specialized, as is the case with corporate staff functions, communication patterns and reporting relationships have to be established that will permit efficient information transfer and discussion with minimum pyramiding.

Decisions on how to organize are also affected by management development objectives. Often the design of a subsystem within the organization is tailored for someone the company is grooming for other positions in the structure. One company's decision to form separate profit centers, with general managers responsible for major product lines, was motivated in large part by its desire to utilize its high performers in the most effective manner. Designing structures that are flexible enough to permit both vertical and horizontal mobility should be fundamental to any organization design.

The following questions can be used as guidelines for analyzing the company's management resources and determining their appropriateness to its existing structure or a proposed new structure.

- Is the company's management qualified to support the existing/proposed structure? Are deficiencies or strengths limited to specific businesses the company is in or are the shortages more general?

- If new functions result from reorganization, does the company have the necessary expertise to assume the responsibility?

- Do the company's structural needs call for functional experts, general managers, or both?

- Does the current or proposed structure present key positions that can be used for management or professional development? If so, at what levels do they exist within the structure?

- What key positions within the company's structure are blocked by incumbents who are only average performers?

- What key positions within the structure require highly specialized knowledge and skills?

- Should any positions be created for top performers who are highly promotable?

- Are the company's management resources varied enough to warrant different kinds of structural forms (such as matrix, line, and staff)?

- What is the ratio of managers to supervisors? Supervisors to employees? Managers to professionals? Senior professionals to new professionals? Senior managers to middle managers? How do these ratios compare with those in like businesses?

- What are the demographics of the company's management and professional ranks in terms of age, sex, race, education, and technical specialization experience?

- In what areas should the company develop existing personnel for key positions and in what areas should it recruit from outside its ranks?

Structural considerations should not be bound by the company's management resource limitations. However, decisions related to when to restructure often depend on the organization's capacity to beef up its management and professional resources in order to staff the structure in the most effective manner. Also, decisions on how to position people within the structure depend on the breadth and depth of resources needed to make the organization function productively.

Summary

The primary function of any organizational structure is to provide an integrative mechanism for bringing together the organization's resources to achieve management's objectives. The choice of a given structure should be guided by the company's strategy, technology, and policies. The alignment of relationships within the structure should be based on the communication patterns necessary for effective information processing and decision making as well as on the management resources available to the organization. By analyzing these elements thoroughly and designing structures that flow logically out of this analysis with care, organizations can increase their productivity. Good organization brings order to disorder, reduces conflicts between people over work and responsibility, and helps create an environment conducive to good teamwork.

The five elements listed at the beginning of this chapter provide a framework for both analyzing and designing organizational structures. When designing the overall structure of an organization, it is important to analyze each of these elements. In designing the subunits within the overall structure, the analytical process usually includes only an examination of policy, communication patterns, and management resources. However, statements of policy usually are designed from specific statements of functional or operational strategy.

In this chapter I have attempted to outline an alternative approach that can involve managers in the total process of analyzing and designing the structure of the function for which they are responsible. To gain optimum effectiveness and efficiency from the company's basic management tool—organizational structure—management will have to become more involved in the process of analyzing structure just as it has played an expanding role in other important areas of the business.

7

Implementing
organizational change

WHEN CHANGES in structure or roles are introduced into an organization there is inevitable conflict. This conflict often affects basic organizational processes necessary to sustain the ongoing business environment. Just as the human system passes through several phases as it adapts to physiological and psychological changes, people in organizations pass through social and psychological phases when changes are introduced within their work environment.

I have previously discussed the notion that most major organizational studies are conducted by outside management consultants who normally do not concern themselves with the behavioral implication of change. Once having recommended a structure, these consultants often leave the important task of implementing the structure to managers who, because they have not participated in either the analysis or the design stage of the study, are often ill equipped to explain the rationale or implications of the change. What are the psychological effects?

Stephen L. Fink has identified* four psychological phases people go through when they are faced with an unexpected change

* "Crisis and Motivation," *Archives of Physical Medicine and Rehabilitation*, vol. 49, 1967.

that disrupts normal conditions and/or normal behavior patterns. He refers to these phases as shock, defensive retreat, acknowledgment, and adaptation and change.

Shock phase

During this stage the person comes to the realization that his or her existing structure or modus operandi is in real danger. Normal organizational procedures are disrupted. People are tentative and confused. Self-preservation becomes the No. 1 issue. Because people cannot fully grasp what is happening, their coping mechanisms do not function adequately. They are often left with feelings of helplessness, intensive anxiety, and even panic.

Defensive retreat phase

Anxiety during the shock phase leads people into fight or flight behavior during this phase. Because employees have great difficulty tolerating what is happening, they attempt to fortify the habitual and familiar structure so as to shut out or control the threat imposed by the change. They try to convince themselves that things have not really changed by clinging to the past. Reality is avoided or denied, and they are likely to indulge in wishful thinking. Their thinking becomes rigid and they typically refuse to consider the possibility of change in any aspect of their life-styles, values, or goals.

Acknowledgment phase

Eventually the defenses are destined to break down, because the sources of support begin to fail. Slowly, employees discover that some of their values and ways of coping with the world are no longer successful. There is a renewed encounter with reality and, consequently, a renewed period of stress. The feeling state that accompanies these changes is one of depression. There is a sense of loss and often an attitude of bitterness. On a cognitive level, a breakdown of organized, planned thinking occurs. This is followed by the beginnings of a reorganization in terms of altered reality perceptions.

Adaptation and change phase

People begin to modify their self-image and develop a renewed sense of worth. New satisfactions are experienced, and with these anxiety and depression decrease. Thinking and planning are organized in terms of present resources and future potentials. The overall picture is one in which people cope successfully with their world and no longer consider themselves to be in a state of crisis or change.

These phases are inevitable and sequential when major changes in organizational structure or role occur; every member affected by the change will pass through these phases in his or her own manner. The amount of shock experienced will, of course, depend on the extent to which the employee is affected by the change. The degree to which he or she retreats from the reality of the change will depend on such factors as personal makeup, predisposition to accept change, likes and dislikes of the change, and understanding of the implications of the change. The amount of time it takes that person to acknowledge and adapt to the change will depend on some of these same factors.

Although Fink's model applies to people who experience a personal crisis (it evolved primarily from people who had experienced personal tragedies such as the loss of a loved one or a physical tragedy), it can also be used to describe the psychological impact of an organizational change. When members in an organization perceive that the work unit to which they belong and upon which they depend could be eliminated or substantially changed, they experience a form of crisis similar to a personal tragedy or the loss of a loved one. The reaction to an organizational change is not likely to be as severe as, for example, the loss of eyesight or a limb, but the psychological phases through which the individual passes are the same; the individual does, in fact, experience a type of crisis. In the same sense, an organization is in a state of crisis when any segment critical to its total function is threatened.

There is a cost associated with organizational change that is often unrecognized or ignored by management. As people begin to anticipate organizational changes or when changes are introduced unexpectedly, the basic processes of the business—planning, decision making, leadership, communications, problem solving, and implementation—are dramatically affected. Let's examine these effects further.

Planning

During an anticipated or announced major organizational change, planning and goal setting often stagnate until employees acknowledge and adapt to the change. The shock of a major structural realignment or change in top management often causes managers at lower levels in the organization to operate in an automatic fashion; the initial shock of the change makes them unable to formulate any plan of action. Because a realignment usually creates different reporting relationships in the management hierarchy, those affected by the change are less likely to establish new plans or new goals. Their tendency is to wait until the expectations of the new management are known.

As people pass from the shock to the defensive retreat phase, planning and goal setting tend to be done for the sake of expediency. As a result, the quality of the plans suffers and the commitment to present and future goals deteriorates. Those most affected by the change begin to ask if their plans are consistent with the change.

Most people have a healthy amount of emotion invested in the status quo. This investment provides a powerful impetus to continue doing what has been done successfully in the past. When organizational change occurs, employees become less certain of their roles and often stop doing even successful things. Anxiety rises and the future becomes less important than the present. Disorganization occurs until the change is acknowledged. Once the change is acknowledged, employees synthesize its effects and begin to redirect their efforts toward planning and goal setting. The planning process does not become well integrated, however, until people have adapted to the change. The time required to unfreeze the planning process by redirecting energy—from assessing the effects of the change to establishing strategies and goals for the future—can be substantial. The costs associated with this lost planning time, while difficult to calculate, are probably enormous.

Decision Making

Major changes in organizational structure characteristically paralyze ongoing decision making during the shock phase. The new roles brought on by a structural realignment often create an environment of uncertainty about who has the responsibility and authority to make decisions. Subordinates often delay making ordinary decisions until they know the extent to which their new boss is willing to delegate decision making and to support them once they have made a decision.

Decision making tends to be highly autocratic as employees pass from the shock to the defensive retreat phase. The pressures brought on by uncertainty often cause them to postpone decision making. As a result, systems break down, people become less responsive, and information becomes outdated before it is published. During the defensive retreat stage, thinking becomes rigid. There is a tendency to believe that things really haven't changed. Thus decisions that are made during this phase are often based on the past, even though conditions may have changed significantly.

During the acknowledgment phase, decision making tends to become less autocratic and more participative. The employees have begun the process of self-examination and interpersonal confrontation. As the emphasis on interpersonal relations shifts from past to present issues, people begin to perceive each other as resources instead of threats. Decision making then becomes open to a wider range of issues. Commitment to decisions becomes stronger, because more people have had an opportunity to influence the process.

As employees move to the adaptation phase, decisions are made as situations and tasks demand. Energy during this phase is directed primarily at decisions that must be made in order to realize the plans and goals that have been established for the work unit.

The effects of not making decisions during the shock phase and of making decisions with little impact from other organizational members during the defensive retreat phase can be adverse. To move decision making from a state of paralysis to a state of flexibility is often a difficult and time-consuming endeavor.

Leadership

The initial shock of an organizational change causes the leaders affected by the change to become concerned primarily about themselves, which results in fragmented relations between managers and subordinates. A leader's behavior at this stage is likely to be "me" instead of "us" oriented. The normal role of the leader—to make decisions, establish work practices, evaluate subordinate performance, solve day-to-day operational problems—seems irrelevant. The leader's main focus is on the immediate threat to his or her position and power in the hierarchy. Leadership at this stage is chaotic.

The leader's behavior during the defensive retreat phase is likely to be governed by a belief that survival is of the utmost importance. Leaders are preoccupied with the fear of losing control. Their tendency is to establish absolute controls over information flow. They handle problems in mechanical rather than creative ways. Risk taking is avoided. Problems are disposed of rather than solved. Leaders become "now" oriented, emphasizing the necessity of getting the job done today. Tried-and-true solutions are sought. Leadership during this phase is regressive.

The leaders who are willing and able to survive the shock and defensive retreat phases and move into the acknowledgment phase begin to search for new and better ways to communicate with subordinates. During the acknowledgment period, leaders attempt to redefine their roles and to establish or reaffirm their relationships with their superior, peers, and subordinates. Leaders typically doubt the validity of their past practices during this phase and, as new structures and new relationships are tried out, they depend less and less on their past methods and become more attuned to current developments in the organization. Leadership at this stage is experimental.

As leaders adapt to the change, they become more task oriented and once again concern themselves with such matters as resource allocations, planning, and decision making. Their orientation shifts from "me" to "us," and their behavior becomes less experimental and more predictable.

Chaotic, regressive leadership is painfully costly to an organization. Changing structures, shifting tasks, modifying goals, and promoting and/or demoting managers can introduce a measure of shock to an organization. Getting leaders to move from the shock to the adaptation phase requires time, patience, and often retraining—and all of these have their price.

Communications

Of all the basic business processes affected by a major organizational change, communications, both formal and informal, deteriorate most quickly in the shock phase. During this phase, interpersonal relationships become fragmented and disconnected. People do not know how much to disclose or what kinds of information to seek. Communications between individuals and between groups are random and usually without purpose, since the energy required to function effectively as a work unit has been diffused. While the organization is in shock, it is difficult for any useful communication to occur.

As people move from shock to defensive retreat, they begin to turn to each other for therapeutic purposes. Communications become highly selective. People begin to form cohesive groups that are intended to act as shields for self-protection. Useful exchanges of information for problem solving do not occur. Instead, organization members go through the motion of information sharing without really meaning to appraise the implications of the change.

As people begin to acknowledge the change, they start to seek out situations in which they can ask questions, disclose their feelings, and receive feedback from other organization members. The purposes of communication at this phase are to find mutual support and explore common problems. Communications tend to be intensive. People have a high need for information exchange to discover the meaning of the newness brought about by the change. Fear of the implications of the change also tends to create a high level of tension. Written communications proliferate and meetings and private discussions become more numerous and perhaps longer than usual. Real agendas often fall by the wayside.

The communication process changes significantly and people begin to adapt to the change. Communications become more authentic. They are intended to direct attention toward real problems. The need to coordinate and to work interdependently is recognized. Communications stabilize and become dependable.

Changes that disrupt or are perceived to endanger well-established communication relationships cause employees to create systems for reducing or eliminating the anticipated harm. The greater the shock and the longer the period of time it takes to move to the adaptation phase, the greater the chance of people creating communication systems that are counterproductive to the implementation of the change. To unravel and defuse these systems requires analysis, time, and energy that could better be spent in building new communication relationships.

Problem Solving and Implementation

Problem solving during the shock phase does not exist. Problems that are of a day-to-day nature or that occur unexpectedly are overlooked. The implementation of solutions and the activities that must take place to handle situations that demand immediate attention become irrelevant.

After the initial effects of the shock have worn off and people move into the defensive retreat phase, they begin to impose highly structured, risk-adverse solutions and actions to any problem situation. Because the central purpose of behavior during this phase is to maintain the present state of the organization, employees tend to view all problems and all actions from a short-term perspective. Problem solving at this stage is not analytically based. Solutions and actions are standardized, practical, and easy to implement.

During the acknowledgment phase, individuals begin to explore alternative solutions. They do not assume that there are simple formulas for solving problems. They are willing to investigate a range of ideas from those that are highly conceptual to those that are routinely practical. As a result, solutions and actions become more attuned to the problems under consideration. The commitment to solutions is not yet high, however. People still haven't gained each other's confidence and support. The acknowledgment phase is characterized by testing, weighing, validating, trial, and uncertainty.

Problems are delegated to the people best equipped to solve them after everyone has adapted to the change. Premature action is the exception rather than the rule. Problems are subjected to thorough examination before solutions are offered. Problem solving and implementation are highly adaptive.

Table 4. Business processes during four phases.

	Planning	Decision making	Leadership	Communications	Problem Solving
Shock	Stagnation	Paralysis	Chaotic	Random	Nonexistent
Defensive retreat	Expediency	Autocratic	Regressive	Self-protective	Standardized
Acknowledgment	Redirection	Participative	Experimental	Intensive	Trial and Error
Adaption and change	Redirected	Situational	Predictive	Authentic	Adaptive

The absence of problem solving during the shock phase, the lack of analysis at the defensive retreat phase, and the unwillingness to commit oneself at the acknowledgment phase can have adverse effects upon an organization over both the short and the long run. Decisions made at the defensive retreat phase often haunt the organization for months and even years. Ineffective or deficient problem solving is costly at best, destructive at worst. The various stages are delineated in Table 4.

Summary

A significant problem with most organizational studies is that they often ignore people's response to change, at great expense to the company. It is not uncommon for management to spend substantial sums analyzing structural or policy issues through the efforts of outside (and, in more recent years, inside) consultants and very little time or money on the critical issues of gaining understanding, acceptance, and commitment to the changes proposed in the study. In many companies, major changes are introduced to organization members by means of substandard written communications that announce new reporting relationships or new job titles. The critical question of how to manage the behavior of people toward the change is rarely asked and almost never answered.

Changes in organizations can be introduced efficiently and effectively if management understands what happens to people during the change process. Knowledge of important behavioral science principles can shorten the phases of shock and defensive retreat and move employees into the acknowledgment and adaptation phases much sooner. In the next chapter we will examine how one company organized and managed a major change in its organization with little disruption to itself.

8

How to implement organizational change

MOST ATTEMPTS to change organizational structure or to reduce overhead costs alienate middle and lower levels of management from top management. Faced with the reality that top management is "going to do something to them," managers below the
top levels of management often remain in the defensive retreat
phase for long periods of time while someone employed by the
company's senior executive journeys through the organization collecting and assimilating information.

In many instances, top management places a veil of secrecy
around organizational studies by releasing written notices to managers that are designed to conceal the real purpose of the studies.
These notices frequently contain phrases such as "In our continuous attempts to improve our management effectiveness we have
employed the *XYZ* firm to help us in planning the company's future," or "Because our recent performance as a company suggests
that we need to improve in certain areas, the company has retained the *XYZ* firm to identify improvement opportunities." Such
communications go on to encourage managers to cooperate with
the firm the company has employed by answering any questions it
might ask or by providing it with the information it will need to
conduct its analysis.

This approach may be intended to cause minimal disruption to the business and to reduce people's anxiety about possible organizational changes, but its real impact is quite the opposite. Rather than feeling that they are integral parts of an organizational change effort, managers are more likely to feel that top management doesn't trust them with important information and is unwilling to involve them in the conceptual or hard issues facing the company.

Where a large-scale reorganization or cost reduction effort involving a major portion of the company's management is intended, misrepresenting the real purpose of an organizational study can seriously affect top management's credibility with lower levels of management. The surest way to impede planning, decision making, leadership, communications, problem solving, and implementation and to reinforce defensive behaviors is to camouflage an organizational change effort with catchy phrases or half truths. The company's grapevine will decipher and disseminate these, in its own terms, and often to the company's detriment, throughout the organization.

What, then, is the alternative? Should top management be completely candid about the intent of an organizational study? To what extent can managers become involved in a study that might, in fact, affect their position in the organization? The answers to these questions are explored within the context of an approach that can be used to bring about organizational changes with minimal disruption.

Staff Productivity Study

In the past decade, many corporations have moved to organize their staff functions into highly specialized departments in order to improve their quality of information, services, and systems. This improvement effort usually includes the creation of a number of new staff functions and a significant upgrading of many existing

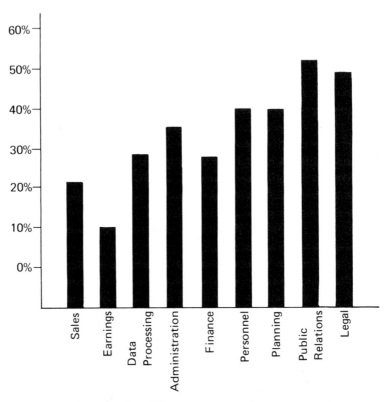

Figure 11. Growth of staff functions over a five-year period.

functions. A lot of these companies have followed a pattern of recruiting heavily from outside their ranks for top- and middle-level
executives to manage these functions. Figure 11 shows the staff's
growth, measured in expense over time, for one such company.
The rate of growth of staff departments significantly surpassed the
rate of growth in sales and profits over a five-year period. Top
management often accepts this growth because it infers future returns on investment in people, systems, and procedures. These returns, however, don't always materialize.

The rapid increase in the size of staff departments and the accompanying new requirements for reports, programs, and other information from line management often create major problems between operating and staff personnel. The problem can intensify to the point where line personnel label staff departments "unnecessary overhead," "spies," and "menacing intruders" while staff personnel label line managers "backward," "shortsighted," and "unsystematic."

One way to address the problems of staff productivity and line–staff relations is for top management to form a study team to analyze (1) the effectiveness of the staff organizational structure, (2) the efficiency of staff service efforts, and (3) the interpersonal relationships between line and staff personnel. To accomplish these purposes, the study should be designed in three phases.

Phase one

The first phase of the study involves the formation of a study team consisting of people from inside the company and, preferably, an external consultant. The study team should be chartered with the responsibility of analyzing the structure and identifying the specific problem areas between line and staff personnel. The specific objectives of phase one of the study are as follows:

To identify the principal roles of the staff service departments as specified in the company's charter or policy statements.
To describe the specific responsibilities of each department as these responsibilities are viewed by incumbent managers.
To identify the users of staff services.

The study team should begin its analysis by focusing on the company's stated policies for each of the functional areas. After carefully analyzing the written documents, the team should conduct interviews with the company's senior management, both at the corporate and at the divisional levels (if appropriate) in order to gain management's assessment of what it expects from the company's staff functions. The information from the interviews and from the written statements of charter or policy should be organized into four major roles, defined as follows:

Support to executive management. This category includes all work directly assigned to or routinely done by staff departments for the company's top executives.

Support to line operations. This category includes all work done by staff departments at the request of line operating personnel. The work may be part.of routine or completed as the result of a special request.

Administrative support. This category includes all administrative work that has been centralized for efficiency and is done by staff departments for the corporation.

Audit and control on operations. This category includes all work done by staff departments in developing and implementing policies and programs to verify information or to direct or constrain operating and staff management.

These roles should be communicated to staff managers by calling a special meeting to explain that managers' responsibilities should be thought of within the context of one or more of them. The same meeting can be used to brief managers on the purpose and scope of the study effort. In appealing for their support, top management should make every effort to indicate that all managers will participate in the analysis and interpretation of the results as well as in the implementation of any change.

After reaching agreement with top management on these stated roles for the staff functions, the study team should enlist the support of managers in all departments to analyze the communications and management resources in their respective areas further. This analysis might include the following steps:

1. Each staff manager is asked to identify all the major functional activities in his or her department. Time, manpower, and dollar allocations for each activity should also be calculated.

2. Working with these managers, the study team should divide each activity into one of the four major staff roles: support to executive management, support to line operations, administrative support, and audit and control on operations.

3. The information from steps 1 and 2 should then be consolidated and reported to top management in a format similar to the one shown in Figure 12.

4. The results of the study team analysis should be fed back to each department manager.

The data from phase one will not be conclusive enough to make specific organizational or staff efficiency recommendations, but they are an effective step toward creating an awareness of problem areas. In one department in which this method was followed, almost all of the staff's time was found to be devoted to formulating policy and exercising control on line operations. However the original intent of the function, as conceived by top management, had been to provide consultation and assistance to line operations in an advisory capacity only. In another department, over 80 percent of the staff's time was allocated to conducting research for a few select people in the company whereas the department's charter identified only an audit and control role for this department.

Phase one of the study can succeed in getting every staff manager to specify the nature and scope of services provided by his or her department for the rest of the company. This form of self-analysis enables managers to specify their responsibilities in terms that are consistent with the four major staff roles and to quantify the time and cost associated with their responsibilities. In short, those closest to the problem can be involved in the early stages of the organizational analysis and in fact participate in the collection and organization of the data. Phase one, therefore, provides a descriptive information base of staff responsibilities that serves as a mir-

Department Total Enrollment _____

Department Responsibilities	Executive Support	Line Support	Adminis- trative Support	Audit Control	% of Staff Time Allocated	Actual Cost
A.	☐	☐	☐	☐	☐	☐
B.	☐	☐	☐	☐	☐	☐
C.	☐	☐	☐	☐	☐	☐
D.	☐	☐	☐	☐	☐	☐
E.	☐	☐	☐	☐	☐	☐
F.	☐	☐	☐	☐	☐	☐

Figure 12. Department responsibilities, type of support, and time distribution.

ror—"This is how I see myself"—for staff managers at several levels in the organizational hierarchy.

Phase two

The primary purpose of the second phase of the study is to provide staff service managers with feedback on their service. To develop a representative list of users, each manager is asked to identify the people in the company who they perceive to be *primary* users of the staff services identified in phase one of the study. In some instances the user lists might consist of a random sample of employees; in other cases, they might be comprehensive lists of all users.

A questionnaire listing the service activities should then be prepared and distributed to all users. Figure 13 is representative of the type of questionnaire distributed. It should be so designed as to require each recipient to judge his need and satisfaction for each departmental responsibility. In this example, respondents were asked to judge three components of satisfaction for each activity —timeliness, thoroughness, accuracy. The design of the questionnaire is intended to represent the actual work done by the department and to give the staff service manager an index of the effectiveness of his or her efforts as well as to suggest how activities might be redesigned to enhance their efficiency and productivity.

To supplement questionnaire results follow-up interviews with a random sample of users may be advisable. The primary objectives of these interviews are to identify user understanding of the questionnaire and to gain insight into the rationale for many of their responses.

Based on the information collected from this questionnaire, a written report for top management and for each staff head should be prepared. The report will indicate how the users viewed each major staff activity in terms of their needs and their levels of satisfaction. The report should also suggest an action plan (phase three) for communicating and taking action on the results.

Name _____   Remember: 1 = Low, 7 = High

Department Responsibility	Frequency of contact	Need	Accuracy	Satisfaction Thoroughness	Timeliness
Labor Relations					
Contract negotiations	☐ ☐	☐ ☐	☐ ☐	☐ ☐	☐ ☐
Grievance handling					
Staffing					
Executives and managers	☐ ☐ ☐	☐ ☐ ☐	☐ ☐ ☐	☐ ☐ ☐	☐ ☐ ☐
Nonsupervisory personnel					
Internal placements					
Training and Development					
Managers and supervisors	☐ ☐ ☐	☐ ☐ ☐	☐ ☐ ☐	☐ ☐ ☐	☐ ☐ ☐
Professionals					
Nonsupervisory personnel					
Compensation and Job Analysis					
Executives and managers	☐ ☐ ☐	☐ ☐ ☐	☐ ☐ ☐	☐ ☐ ☐	☐ ☐ ☐
Professionals					
Nonsupervisory personnel					
Benefits Administrations	☐	☐	☐	☐	☐
Employee Publications	☐	☐	☐	☐	☐

Figure 13. Example questionnaire for users.

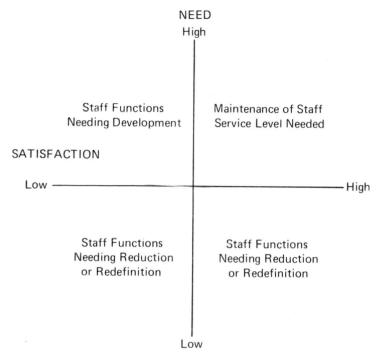

Figure 14. Model for examining function levels.

Phase three

Phase three of this organizational change effort starts with discussions among the staff heads as to how the results of the analysis can serve as a basis for improving the output in their functional areas. The grid shown as Figure 14 is suggested as a model to follow for examining their functions.

These discussions can be pursued with managers below the functional heads. Sometimes when this approach has been used, departments have been eliminated or managers replaced before discussions at lower levels occurred. However, in most instances, the responsibility for improving the level of staff service was placed in the hands of each manager. The managers have taken various steps. They have cut back their services, reduced corporate staff personnel, and sometimes eliminated reports, procedures, and systems that senior management and/or operating management felt were not needed. In other cases they have sought additional information from their users, particularly when a service fell in the high-need/low-satisfaction quadrant. In a few cases, managers have added staff or changed procedures to improve the quality of the service. These actions can follow only if the data are collected, analyzed, and fed back to staff managers for their use in making both structural and efficiency changes.

With some assistance from a study team, staff managers can achieve significant reductions in the level of service to their users without negatively affecting company performance. Also, by reducing unnecessary reports, programs, procedures, or other services, staff managers are able to reduce their annual operating budgets. To achieve these results, several communication meetings should be held with staff managers, line personnel, and top management. Input on matters related to the questions "How can we improve our efficiency?" and "What is the optimum way to organize?" can be obtained by the study team from multiple organizational levels. Where reorganizations and/or reductions in personnel or services do occur, they should be explained carefully to all employees in one-on-one and group sessions.

Because changes in organization affect other company systems and procedures, ad hoc task forces can be formed to rewrite job descriptions, redefine position levels, establish new job titles, write new functional policy statements, reformulate future plans and objectives for each functional work unit, and, where appropriate, relocate people or departments.

Throughout phase three, managers at all organizational levels are involved in helping to implement both the changes recommended by the study team and the changes they initiated on their own, based on the information provided them from phases one and two of the study. Implementation should not be left to the study team alone or to chance. Rather, it should be a total management responsibililty.

Behavioral Principles

Although it is not possible to avoid the psychological trauma associated with organizational change completely, the entire change process can be managed with minimum disruption to the business. It is important to recognize five behavioral science principles and to use them to guide both the analysis and the implementation of change in organization.

1. *The amount of opposition to change is reduced when those who are most affected by the change participate in the design, execution, interpretation, and planning stages of the process.*

Change that comes from within the organization is less threatening and results in less opposition than change that is mandated as a result of analytical work done outside the management hierarchy. Of course, there are varying degrees of involving managers in studies. These range from complete participation in the process by all managers and supervisors to participation by only the executive responsible for the function.

A good deal of evidence from behavioral studies shows a high correlation between participation and acceptance. Although participation may not always increase the acceptance of organizational changes, it does reduce the amount of overt opposition. The use of a study team and the continued involvement of managers in the process serve the purpose of establishing ownership in information collected and in the actions that follow. Change will still be resisted, but the resistance can be dealt with as part of the whole change effort. Those who oppose change are not ignored or punished for their views. Rather, by virtue of their roles as managers, they become an integral part of the data collection, data feedback, and decision-making processes.

2. *Information that explains the rationale for change must be shared widely in the organization's hierarchy.*

To manage the change well you must manage the communications about the change well. These communications should include specific information on the progress of the study, the potential consequence of the change, and other pertinent data. With this approach, managers are involved in the design of the communications plan, receive frequent updates on the study's progress, and are encouraged to communicate at frequent intervals with employees in their department.

3. *Changes in the way the organization behaves can be brought about by providing specific information to those in decision-making roles about their own effectiveness and about the effectiveness of the people they are responsible for managing.*

This statement is valid provided that the information given to the decision maker is new, objective, and different from the view that may commonly be held. In this approach, the information focuses on the user's perception of the specific responsibilities of the department rather than on general attitudes toward the department. The responsibilities are identified and verified by each department's management. The questionnaire design is influenced significantly by the departments, and user lists are developed by the manager responsible for specific activities. Thus, the information fed back to management is directed toward its desires and at its behavior.

4. *In order to gain maximum acceptance or minimum opposition to an organizational change, decision makers affected by the change must feel that they can benefit personally as a result of the change.*

The design of this study takes into consideration the needs, beliefs, and attitudes of those affected by the change. This is done by giving each manager an opportunity to voice his or her views and thus influence the objectives, design, analysis, interpretation, and communication strategy of the study. The rationale and action plan for improving or eliminating staff services is developed by the management of each department, thereby ensuring an effective link between the objectives of the study and the personal objectives of those being studied.

5. *The higher the credibility of the decision maker, the greater the influence he or she can have on the change process.*

Before the study is initiated, the study team should be assured by top management that each department executive is in good standing—that no terminations or resignations are anticipated. In most hierarchies, the expectations of the top management are generally the most important organizational force for creating change.

Summary

This approach demonstrates that with an understanding of some basic behavioral science principles, management can introduce change into its organization effectively and efficiently. In each phase of the study management is made aware of the behavioral implications of change that can help it to change current business practices

With a knowledge of the behavioral principles of change, management can lessen or alleviate the negative behaviors that are normally manifested during the shock and defensive retreat phases. Following these principles will also shorten the impact of shock and defensive retreat phases and thereby move management and employees into the acknowledgment and adaptation phases much sooner. Finally, understanding these principles can give management the confidence to introduce more changes into the organization. Oftentimes management hesitates to introduce needed change because it fears negative repercussions.

For full performance potential, corporations must design methods of analyzing improvement opportunities and develop systems to implement them. Applying behavioral science principles to the process of change will greatly enhance an organization's capacity to absorb the shock and internalize the expected behaviors. Good management manages change well.

III

Managing for Increased Profitability

Traditional management practices place the full responsibility of corporate profitability on management. Employees, it is argued, have little or no concern for raising productivity, nor should their views be sought regarding ways to improve organization performance. Traditional management often views employees as apathetic or even outright hostile to profitability improvement. To overcome these attitudes, several approaches have been developed over the past few decades aimed at increasing employee motivation. Employee suggestion plans, conventional wage incentives, merit salary increases, and a host of other work-motivation approaches are popular ways of motivating employees to increase productivity.

The work of Douglas McGregor and Frederick Herzberg, two contemporary behavioral scientists, has led to a new approach to problems associated with employee motivation. McGregor's concepts, as refined by Herzberg, argue that management should strive to enrich jobs and provide employees with opportunities to participate in decisions. The two men reason that money is not a motivator; only the work itself provides motivation.

Although some companies have had a limited success with various behavioral approaches aimed at improving employee motivation and productivity, few managers have implemented the ideas of McGregor or others who advocate employee participation in the management process. A recent study on worker motivation, productivity, and job satisfaction conducted by the National Science Foundation pinpointed the major shortcomings of the behavioral approaches to improving productivity in America. The study concluded that the ". . . key to having workers who are both satisfied and productive is motivation." Motivation was defined by the researcher as "arousing and maintaining the will to work effectively—having workers who are productive not because they are coerced but because they are committed." Of all the factors that contribute to a highly motivated workforce, ". . . the principal one appears to be that effective performances be recognized and rewarded—in whatever terms are meaningful to the individual, be it financial or psychological or both.

With the productivity of the American worker slipping at an alarming rate, organizations are faced with the challenge of understanding how to motivate today's employee. The emergence of a new workforce, the subject of Chapter 9, has placed an additional responsibility on executive management to improve its methods of selecting and developing managers, assessing employee attitudes, building organizational teamwork, and at the same time continuing the process of introducing changes that are needed to improve corporate profitability.

Traditional management practices are no longer sufficient to sustain and improve employee performance. If the American free enterprise system is to succeed, executive management must instill the kind of management philosophy that seeks to discover the kinds of psychological and financial rewards that are meaningful to today's employee.

This section identifies the motivational factors that are important to employees in today's work environment. It also offers some suggestions on how to achieve greater organizational profitability by implementing management practices that will lead to a meaningful recognition and reward system for individuals and for teams.

9

The emergence of the "contemporary employee"

FOR SEVERAL YEARS, many of us in the behavioral sciences have been stirred by a vision of an organization whose employees would have, throughout their working lives, opportunities to expand their minds, enlarge their skills, enrich their experience, and fulfill their personal and career needs. In recent years this vision has been shared, at least in part, by a number of top-management officials who have begun to allocate substantial financial resources to the development of their companies' human resources. But the purpose and result of the majority of personal development programs offered by business and industry have remained vague. Little effort has been made to determine the learning needs of the organization, and even less effort has been devoted to evaluating the payoff of most programs.

The growth of company-initiated development programs has been paralleled by an increase in the volume of educational activity aimed at the American adult population. The National Center for Education Statistics concludes that over 17 million adult Americans are currently involved in educational or learning activities associated with their jobs, churches, colleges and universities, or other private or public agencies. Forty million adult Americans are in career transition. The majority of these will participate in some form of career-related education or training.

This increased interest in and commitment to education is further evidenced by the number of different approaches to learning that have come to education in the past ten years: universities without walls, continuing adult education, computer-assisted instruction, nontraditional study, contract learning, weekend college, experimental learning, external degrees, free universities, recurrent education, and so on.

The response of business and industry to these rapid changes has not been casual. More than 20 percent of the people in the workforce have fringe benefits to support advanced learning. And it is not uncommon for organizations to staff departments with professional educators who can offer employees assistance with such services as:

Education and career-planning information
Financial-assistance information
Learning assessment
Professional growth and development
Program planning and development
Program evaluation

The complexity of today's society means that people can gain access to a myriad of educational and developmental opportunities. The increasing level of educational opportunities has created a whole set of employee expectations. No longer does the employee's training and development for job advancement depend on conventional educational programs. Employees with several years of business experience can now obtain advanced degrees, professional certification, or increased technical skills through weekend, evening, correspondence, or individually tailored educational programs. The years of experience, coupled with this advanced development, allow employees to reexamine career objectives and advancement opportunities and the content and pay of their current positions.

Organizations are now challenged to advance from a general affirmation and enthusiasm about personal career development to a maturer stage. The general concepts and goals of industry's education and development programs must be made more precise. They must be better and more widely understood, reflected in formal policy statements, and translated into institutional and personal practice.

Just as the company's planning function must explore future economic scenarios and their implications for business growth and development, education and personnel development functions must explore alternative futures and their implications for learning. What will the shape of America's future be? How will our society change within the next five, ten, or fifteen years—in the ways people work, live, behave, communicate, and learn? These questions must be explored as an integral part of an organization's human resource development strategy.

The rapid rise in the level of educational sophistication has been accompanied by a dramatic change in the values of the workforce. This change has created, and will continue to create, the need for a new kind of management. The change, and the kind of management required to motivate today's employee, must be elucidated. We will try to do so in the remainder of this section.

Changing Values

Changes in the expectations and values of the workforce are a reality. A good deal of research suggests that younger workers have different attitudes toward work than their predecessors. Of equal importance is the fact that these new attitudes appear to be spreading to older members of the workforce. How widespread are these attitudinal differences and how do they affect the management process? The demographics of the present workforce provide a partial answer to this question. According to the *Employment and Training Report of the President* (1978) approximately one-half of the workforce is under age 34. The number of people employed in professional occupations has doubled in the past 20 years, while the number of managerial employees has increased by one-third during this same period. In addition, more and more young people are enrolled in colleges and universities. In 1957, only 7 percent of the civilian workforce had completed four or more years of higher education. By 1977, this figure had risen to almost 17 percent.

Women are entering the job market at an increasing rate and are holding jobs that were traditionally held by men. The number of women who have completed at least four years of college has increased by more than 6 percent in the past 20 years. Opportunities for women and minorities are increasing at an accelerated rate, owing to such factors as the advent of the Equal Employment Opportunity Commission.

Traditional work values

But the demographics speak only to one part of the change. In the past several years there has been a dramatic shift in the personal values held by the workforce. Traditional employees defined their identity through their work role. Personal desires that conflicted with this role were usually subordinated or suppressed. The fundamental purpose of work was to provide the individual with enough money to meet family obligations. Employees were tied to their jobs by commitments to their family and by loyalty to the organization. Money and status were used as basic incentives for motivating employees. An integral part of every person's role was to please the organization. Thus, a steady full-time job with adequate compensation was viewed as a highly desirable goal.

The traditional employee regarded hierarchy and authority with esteem. Typically, employees learned their skill at the expense of the company. Promotions were based on years of experience and loyalty to the company. Employees were strongly oriented to seek and accept direction from those above them in the hierarchy. Deviations from authority were rare. Employees were likely to put up with such company demands as long hours, frequent moves, and tedious, routine work, as long as their identities as good family providers could be preserved. The fundamental work value of traditional employees was to obtain and hold a job that would enable them to fulfill their economic obligations.

Contemporary work values

Contemporary employees are committed to a different set of values. Their self-esteem is not intricately interwoven with economic or familial obligations. They are more individualistic. Loyalty to the organization is secondary to personal loyalty. Contemporary employees feel responsible primarily to themselves. Authority and organizational hierarchy are not held in high regard. The uncertainty of the future is of little concern; what counts is what happens today.

Contemporary employees have a desire for immediate advancement. They demand challenging nonroutine work and a voice in the organization's decision-making process. They are motivated by participation in setting goals and by rewards that are linked directly to their accomplishments. Communication, particularly as it relates to feedback, encouragement, and recognition, is very important to them. The opportunity to influence both co-worker and management is equally important.

Contemporary employees are more ambitious and independent than traditional employees. They have less respect for authority and are generally less willing to do what they are told. Because contemporary employees are more likely to be trained for their po-

sitions away from the company, they do not feel as great a sense of
obligation to the company as their predecessors. Therefore, they
are more likely to place demands on the organization for challenging, creative work and for promotional opportunities.
Lauren Jackson, after an extensive review of the research that
compares and contrasts traditional and contemporary work values,
offers the following conclusions:*

> The traditional employee displayed more loyalty and commit-
> ment to the company than the contemporary employee.
> Compensation has always been an important value to employ-
> ees, but it tends to be valued more as a consequence of per-
> formance by contemporary employees.
> Contemporary employees are more concerned with recognition
> than traditional employees.
> Contemporary employees have more desire to participate in
> decisions that affect them.
> Traditional employees are more concerned with job security.
> Contemporary employees value communication from manage-
> ment about what's going on in the company.
> Contemporary employees have more short-term goal orienta-
> tion, as opposed to traditional employees, who have more
> long-term goal orientation.
> More than traditional employees, the contemporary group de-
> sires its work to be challenging.
> Contemporary employees are more concerned that their work
> be worthwhile.
> Contemporary employees desire developmental opportunities.
> Contemporary employees want their work to be interesting.
> Contemporary employees want their work to be creative.
> The traditional employee puts work before family and leisure.
> The contemporary employee places family first—then leisure
> and work.

* Unpublished dissertation.

Analyzing Managerial Values

Motivating the contemporary employee requires a different form of management. Recognizing and adapting to employees who hold different work values from those of the past are among the greatest challenges facing management. Managers who have the capacity to understand how work values and managerial styles combine to motivate today's employee will be sought after. In order to motivate both traditional and contemporary employees, managers must be aware of the differences in work values. Equally important, managers must be aware of their own values. The questionnaire shown as Figure 15 can be used by managers to assess their own orientation toward employee motivation. Although the questions included represent only a sample of those in the "Inventory of Managerial Values" developed by Mark Mindell and myself, enough are cited to indicate value tendencies.

Interpreting the Inventory

This inventory measures five major value dimensions: locus of control, self-esteem, tolerance of ambiguity, social judgment, and need for dependency. By reviewing the explanations of each of these dimensions, it is possible to obtain an indication of value preference. The explanations are presented using the "ideal manager" as a frame of reference and the terms "contemporary" and "traditional" to dichotomize value orientation. Although no manager is exclusively "contemporary" or "traditional," each has a basic value orientation that strongly influences management behavior. The inventory should be viewed within this context.

Locus of control

The ideal manager holding either contemporary or traditional values believes that there is a strong connection between his efforts

Figure 15. Inventory of managerial values.

A number of descriptions of personal characteristics related to the process of management are listed here. These descriptions are followed by a scale ranging from "1," which indicates strong disagreement, to "7," which indicates strong agreement.

When completing the survey, please circle the number that best represents your personal feeling regarding the statement. Remember, the higher numbers indicate agreement, the lower numbers indicate disagreement.

1. As a manager, I function *best* in unstructured, somewhat ambiguous stituations.

   Strongly Disagree   1   2   3   4   5   6   7   **Strongly Agree**

2. There is usually no such thing as an organizational problem that cannot be solved.

   Strongly Disagree   1   2   3   4   5   6   7   **Strongly Agree**

3. There is usually one right way of doing things.

   Strongly Disagree   1   2   3   4   5   6   7   **Strongly Agree**

4. When organizations are successful, it is usually due more to chance than to systematic planning.

   Strongly Disagree   1   2   3   4   5   6   7   **Strongly Agree**

5. When people advance in the organization it is often because of who they know rather than what they do.

   Strongly Disagree   1   2   3   4   5   6   7   **Strongly Agree**

6. As a manager, I have a great deal of influence over how people behave in the organization.

   Strongly Disagree   1   2   3   4   5   6   7   **Strongly Agree**

7. I exercise a great deal of self-control in my position as manager.

   Strongly Disagree   1   2   3   4   5   6   7   **Strongly Agree**

8. It is important to provide frequent feedback to employees regarding how well they are performing.

Strongly Disagree   1   2   3   4   5   6   7   Strongly Agree

9. My ideas are usually understood and accepted.

Strongly Disagree   1   2   3   4   5   6   7   Strongly Agree

10. Most people in an organization work because they have to, not because they want to.

Strongly Disagree   1   2   3   4   5   6   7   Strongly Agree

11. It is often necessary to step on some toes in order to get the job done.

Strongly Disagree   1   2   3   4   5   6   7   Strongly Agree

12. People in the organization often let their feelings get in the way of business.

Strongly Disagree   1   2   3   4   5   6   7   Strongly Agree

13. I am concerned about where I will be in the company in five years.

Strongly Disagree   1   2   3   4   5   6   7   Strongly Agree

14. I have a high degree of loyalty to my company.

Strongly Disagree   1   2   3   4   5   6   7   Strongly Agree

15. Job security is very important to me.

Strongly Disagree   1   2   3   4   5   6   7   Strongly Agree

---

to manage and the success of the organization. Both types of managers feel that they have control over events through their managerial decisions. They believe that success cannot be left up to chance but must be planned and monitored. They also believe that advancement depends on achievement rather than political affiliation and that they have a great deal of influence over how people behave in the organization.

Items 4, 5, and 6 represent three measures of the locus-of-control dimension. The ideal manager holding contemporary and/or traditional values would have a high locus of control and would strongly disagree with items 4 and 5 and strongly agree with item 6.

Self-esteem

The ideal contemporary and traditional manager should have the capacity to provide recognition of employee accomplishments with feedback that preserves and enhances individual self-esteem. Managers who are able to exercise self-control, who feel that their ideas are creative, understood, and accepted, and who feel that feedback to employees regarding' their performance is important, tend to have high self-esteem. Managers who believe that employees cannot be trusted, who lack confidence in people, who have a tendency to be critical, annoyed, or irritated by people with different ideas or values, tend to score low on self-esteem.

Items 7, 8, and 9 are examples of the items that make up the self-esteem dimension. The ideal manager holding contemporary and/or traditional values would score high on self-esteem and would strongly agree with items 7, 8, and 9.

Tolerance of ambiguity

Managers holding contemporary values have the ability and often the desire to function in unstructured and somewhat ambiguous situations. They have almost a fantasylike view that no problem is so large or complex that it cannot be solved if they put their mind to it. Their tendency is to experiment with a variety of ideas because they believe strongly that there is more than one right way of doing things.

Items 1, 2, and 3 are partial measures of the ambiguity dimension. The ideal manager of employees holding contemporary values would strongly agree with items 1 and 2 and would strongly disagree with item 3. The opposite or near-opposite view would characterize the ideal manager of employees holding traditional values.

Social judgment

Social perceptiveness, sensitivity, empathy, social intelligence, and social insight characterize the manager with contemporary values. Since contemporary employees value good interpersonal relations and personal recognition based on accomplishment highly, it is important for them to work for a manager who displays a high concern for these values. The contemporary manager believes that it is possible to create an environment in which people work because they want to rather than need to; in which worker feelings contribute rather than detract from task accomplishment; and in which positive rewards rather than punitive actions are used to get the job done.

Items 10, 11, and 12 represent examples of questions used to measure managerial social judgment tendencies. The ideal manager of employees holding contemporary values would strongly disagree with each of these statements. Managers holding more traditional values would tend to agree with these statements, since they need to display social judgment characteristics only in moderate proportions.

Need for dependency

Managers who enjoy taking chances and who seek excitement and change are more likely to have contemporary values than managers who are highly cautious, who consider matters very carefully before making decisions, and who do not like to take chances or run risks. Contemporary managers are likely to act in ways that might be regarded by traditional managers as impulsive, erratic, or spur of the moment. Since their dependency needs typically are low, they are more concerned about the present and the

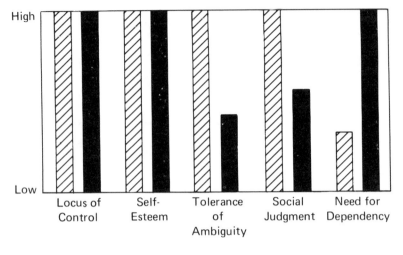

Figure 16. Comparison of ideal contemporary manager and ideal traditional manager.

immediate future than about their long-term careers. They are loyal first to their own needs and desires, and second to the needs and desires of the organization of which they are a part. They are only moderately concerned about job security.

Items 13, 14, and 15 are measures of the need-for-dependency dimension. The ideal manager of employees holding contemporary values would show only a moderate degree of agreement with item 13, would disagree with item 14, and would probably be neutral on item 15. The ideal manager of employees holding traditional values would tend to agree strongly with each of the statements.

Figure 16 compares each of these dimensions in terms of their importance in establishing behavioral patterns for the ideal contemporary and traditional manager. The figure shows that both the ideal contemporary and traditional manager regard locus of control and self-esteem as very important managerial behaviors. Contemporary managers depart significantly from traditional managers in their views of the importance of tolerance of ambiguity, social judgment, and need for dependency.

Summary

Organizations currently employ a mix of contemporary and traditional managers together with a mix of contemporary and traditional employees. When contemporary employees are managed by contemporary managers and traditional employees are managed by traditional managers, the chances of organizational success are greater than when they are integrated. As more and more contemporary employees enter the workforce, there will be an increasing demand for managers who understand and share contemporary values. The need for traditional managers will continue, but their numbers will have to decline to offset the rapid growth of contemporary employees.

How can organizations respond to the increasing and different demands of the workforce? What management mechanisms will have to be put in place to select and develop contemporary leaders, to build and sustain teamwork, to motivate employees, and to introduce innovation within the organization? Making managers aware of their own values is only the first step in a sequence of events that must be put in place to address the challenge of managing today's employee.

To respond successfully to the challenge of managing the emerging contemporary workforce, organizations will have to design and implement new methods for selecting managers, for developing managers, for assessing and responding to employee concerns, for building teamwork, and for increasing management's capacity to introduce change. In the next chapter, a new approach for selecting managers is discussed.

10

Selecting contemporary managers

PERHAPS every influential thinker from Confucius to Bertrand Russell has offered some form of analysis that explains why one person is able to exercise power over another. Earlier studies, such as Plato's *Republic* and the Confucian *Analytics*, examined the concept of leadership by pointing out the ethical and social qualities of good leaders. Aristotle maintained that leaders must be seen as credible, persuasive, and of high moral qualities. Niccolò Machiavelli, in *The Prince*, abstracted certain dynamic principles of successful leadership from history's revelations. However, leadership as such was not studied as a theoretical construct until sociologists and social psychologists began to examine specific traits of leadership as they were observed in business managers.

In his commentary on leadership, Warren Bennis observes that leadership theory is probably the haziest and most confounding area of behavioral study. Bennis further states: ". . . probably more has been written and less is known about leadership than about any other topic in the behavioral sciences." And yet, almost paradoxically, few, if any, subjects are more important to executive management than the selection and development of leaders.

As one looks at the path management theory has taken, it is possible to see two major categories of research findings that contribute at least partially to our understanding and misunderstanding of the qualities of effective managers. The first point of view—usually called the traditional or "trait" approach—identifies certain physical and personality traits that were once thought to be common to all leaders. The second view, to which I will refer as the contemporary approach, rejects the traditional approach while maintaining that management skills can be acquired through training and experience. A closer examination of these two views will help explain the rationale for the approach to selecting and developing managers suggested in this chapter and in Chapter 11.

Traditional Leadership Theory

Douglas McGregor noted that prior to 1930 it was "widely believed that leadership was a property of the individual." A limited number of people were thought to be uniquely endowed with abilities and personality traits that made it possible for them to become leaders, and these qualities were believed to be inherited rather than acquired. Consequently, research studies in this field tended to be directed toward the identification of universal characteristics of leadership so that potential leaders could be identified more easily. What interest there was in such descriptions of leadership behavior during and after the industrial revolution was caught up in a tide of research, most of which took the form of searching for traits of personality that were supposed to characterize the "leader."

R. M. Stogdill provided a review of some earlier studies that attempted to identify specific leadership characteristics. Stogdill's review indicates that a number of studies found leaders to be taller than their subordinates. E. B. Gowin found that executives in insurance companies are taller than policyholders, that bishops are taller than clergymen, that university presidents are taller than college presidents, that sales managers are taller than salesmen, and that railway presidents are taller than station agents.

In addition to the studies examining height as a trait among leaders, other studies looked at physical and constitutional factors such as weight, physique, energy, health, appearance, intelligence, self-confidence, will, dominance, and urgency in an effort to determine the correlation between these factors and leadership ability. Catherine Cox found that great leaders are characterized by such traits as self-confidence, self-knowledge, desire to be in the public eye, physical and mental dominance powers, and an eagerness for admiration. O. W. Caldwell and Beth Wellman found in their study of high school students that in all types of leadership, both girl and boy leaders were more talkative, cheerful, expressive, alert, original, and enthusiastic than nonleaders.

Although many of these earlier studies seemed to suggest that leaders are endowed with certain inherent physical and mental traits that enable them to influence others, Stogdill concludes in his survey that these studies failed to find any consistent pattern of traits that would characterize leaders. Instead, Stogdill contends that the traits of leadership include all or any of the personality (and physical) traits that, in any particular situation, enable a person to direct a group to a recognized goal and to be perceived as doing so by fellow members of a group.

Before the 1930s, the feeling seemed to persist in industrial and business organizations that employees needed a leader who, because of his inherent physical and mental traits, possessed the ability to induce acceptance by others. Influenced greatly by such writers as Max Weber, who believed that strong leadership "makes a man do what he does not want to," business and industrial leaders sought managers at all levels of the organization who, they believed, possessed the necessary traits for being loyal, making decisions, and keeping the workforce in line. This fact may account for some of the reasons research conducted in business and other organizations led to the conclusion that leadership ability was directly related to such variables as physical size and mental abilities, although, as mentioned earlier, most of the research on leadership was conducted in other kinds of settings.

Unfortunately, the traditional approach to selecting managers still exists in many organizations. These organizations have not invested the time and resources required to change their selection process. Numerous interview and other selection guides currently in widespread use within business organizations list only physical and constitutional factors as criteria for assessing candidates for management positions. The traditional approach to selection may have identified managers who could lead traditional employees, those who respond to leaders who demand loyalty, dependency, and commitment to hierarchical rules, but it is irrelevant to the millions in the workforce who hold contemporary values.

Contemporary Leadership Theory

Since 1930 behavioral science research has focused on the study of behavior as well as the physical and constitutional characteristics of leaders. As a result of this research, a number of generalizations about leadership may be made with reasonable certainty.

It is quite unlikely that there is a single basic pattern of abilities and personality traits characteristic of all leaders.

Different situations require different leadership characteristics.

Different functions demand different abilities and skills of leadership.

Many characteristics that have been alleged to be essential to the leader turn out not to differentiate the successful from the unsuccessful leader.

Skills and attitudes can be acquired or modified extensively through learning.

It is apparent that these statements differ markedly from the philosophy of leadership generated by researchers and administrators in the first part of the century. Instead of looking for specific traits in individuals, the "new" view was to examine the phenomenon of leadership as a relationship among the leader, the followers, the characteristics of the organization, and the social and political milieus. The research conducted by contemporary theorists has revealed some interesting and important characteristics of effective leadership.

In the early 1930s, Elton Mayo and his Harvard Business School associates took a different view of the nature of man as he relates to societal organizations. This view, referred to in Chapter 1 as the "human relations approach," took into account such things as the worker's feelings, beliefs, perceptions, ideas, and sentiments. The major assumption of this approach was that man could be motivated to work more productively on the basis of fulfilling certain sociopsychological needs.

Thus, although the manager (leader) is still a key and crucial figure, his role in the organization is much different. Instead of being an autocrat who makes workers do what they do not want to do, he now acts as an agent for maintaining intragroup and intergroup communication and for encouraging wide participation in the decision-making process. This new view of leadership seemed to provoke scholars in a number of different academic disciplines to test some of the assumptions made by Mayo and his associates. The findings of many of the studies that subsequently emerged are the very basis of the generalizations McGregor was able to make about the new theory of leadership.

Chester Barnard viewed leadership in organizations from a functional point of view. The first function of a leader in an organization, according to Barnard, is to serve as a channel of communication insofar as communications must pass through central positions. The second function of the leader is to maintain a system of cooperative effort. The leader must function to direct those actions that are necessary for proper, effective personal adjustment to the environment of the organization. The third function of the leader is to formulate and define the purposes of the organization.

To Barnard, then, the leader is one who can provide the various kinds of services demanded of a management position. In addition to being loyal and responsible, the leader must have specific abilities, such as alertness, flexibility, a range of interests, poise, and specialization in a particular field. Leaders can secure the essential services from employees by bringing people into cooperative relations with the organization and eliciting the services of such people after they have been brought into that relationship. Barnard seems to imply that leaders are gifted with certain physical and personal traits, but he also suggests that the role of the leader in the decision-making process is functional rather than autocratic.

Other scholars interested in the various ways leaders interact with others began to do research on the role of the leader in decision-making groups. Irving Knickerbocker, after surveying the literature on leadership, concludes that "the leader emerges as a consequence of the needs of the group of people and of the nature of the situation within which the group is attempting to operate." Knickerbocker further concludes that leaders are not endowed with magical attributes; rather, leaders arise by performing certain functions related to the needs of the organization.

Knickerbocker reasons that there are four methods a leader may use for directing the activities of people: (1) force, (2) paternalism, (3) bargaining, and (4) mutual means. Of the four, the last is accepted as the best, for it is through this method that the dilemma of the appointed, aggressive, autocratic leader disappears. Thus, to Knickerbocker, the essence of successful leadership in organizations lies in the functional relationship between leaders and followers, a relationship in which management successfully creates the necessary conditions for both the organization and the laborers to work toward common objectives.

In his review of the literature dealing with the problem of the selection of leaders, William Jenkins found that "Leadership is specific to the particular situation under investigation." Jenkins, like Knickerbocker, recognized some of the inadequacies of the literature of leadership and particularly of the traditional researchers' approaches to the subject. Both writers recognized that leadership does not depend on a fixed set of personal characteristics or necessarily on particular kinds of leadership behavior. Instead, they saw it as depending on the circumstances under which groups of people integrate and organize their activities toward objectives and on the way in which that integration and organization is achieved.

The Institute of Social Research at the University of Michigan, as a result of its studies with Prudential Insurance, discovered that leaders using the contemporary approach were likely to be in charge of high-production groups and those characterized by a traditional supervisory style were likely to be in charge of low-production groups. The researchers theorized that the contemporary approach was more effective because supervisors paid greater attention to their employees as human beings and were willing to involve them in the total process of managing.

Other Michigan studies have demonstrated that leaders using the traditional approach are often more effective at achieving increased productivity in the short run, but at a cost of loyalty to the company and interest of employees in their jobs. They also found that traditional leaders had to maintain close surveillance over employees in order to prevent frequent work stoppages. In terms of management style, traditional leaders tended to be defensive, authoritative, and arbitrary, whereas contemporary leaders were more cooperative, democratic, and amenable to reason.

In spite of such findings as these, many top-level executives, and even some researchers in the field of business, still insist on Weber's model of organization led by strong, traditionally oriented leaders. Writing in the *Harvard Business Review* in 1958, Robert McMurry noted that "... managers are hard driving entrepreneurs. Management includes stubbornly destructive people; and, furthermore, only about 10 percent of them *really* believe in the human relations approach." According to McMurry's view, benevolent autocracy gets results because it rigidly structures, routinizes, and controls the relationships between the superior and the subordinate.

In taking this position, McMurry is assuming what men like Taylor and Weber assumed concerning the nature of man;

namely, that man is inherently lazy, uninterested, apathetic, and money crazy, and is constantly creating errors and waste. McMurry's strong autocratic view is much like the nostalgia image of the old-time entrepreneur—the father who is strong, wise, smart, aggressive, and utterly independent. Hence, if any changes are to be made in the organization, this view holds that employees must be changed to cope with the demands of the leader.

In contrast, the contemporary leader shifts the focus from the leader's personality to the dynamics involved in team behavior. A manager's responsibilities are circumscribed by the outlined procedures and delegated responsibilities necessary to achieve the organization's stated goals. Furthermore, since management's accomplishments are dependent on the performance of subordinates, it follows that the effectiveness of the team as a whole is influenced by the manner in which individual team members relate themselves to the manager.

An organization with contemporary leadership philosophy is characterized by many of the following behaviors:

Management solicits subordinates' input regularly at the planning, implementation, and evaluation stages of work.

Management and employees are concerned with a full range of motives, from physical and security needs to social and self-actualization needs.

Information flows freely throughout the system and is free from distortion.

Decision making and control are generally decentralized and occur at all levels through group processes.

Goal setting and performance standards are established and reached through group processes.

People have a sense of working with rather than for others; communication is open and extensive.

The contemporary leadership approach, in the best sense, is an organizationwide effort to create a climate and develop a structure that function participatively. It does not, however, ignore the realities of authority and power. Authority consists of a sphere of control assigned by the organization. A leader's authority is vested in a position legitimatized by a title and a role and backed by the power of the organization. Occasionally contemporary leaders must take advantage of this type of authority. When the authority given to the leader is derived from his technical and managerial competency, that authority stands a much better chance of being well received by subordinates.

Power vested in authority usually refers to the ability to reward or withhold rewards and/or direct punishment in order to assure compliance. Although contemporary leaders must occasionally use power to direct the work of subordinates, they recognize that the most effective way to lead is by influence. Contemporary leaders are cognizant of the fact that authority and power in the modern corporation have very limited scope. Rarely can a person in a position of authority and power manage and secure efficient productivity from subordinates unless he or she can exercise the true role of leadership—influence.

In the past, leaders have been selected for responsible positions in corporations on the basis of how well they relate to the personalities of their superiors rather than how well they relate to other members of the workforce. In the future, leaders will have to be selected and developed based on criteria related more toward contemporary workforce values. How can we assess and develop future contemporary leaders reliably? Let's examine two different approaches that attempt to answer this important question.

Selecting Contemporary Leaders

The question of how to assess leaders reliably has occupied the interests of the academic and business communities for several decades. Since World War II, when the military made extensive use of assessment procedures to select officers, the concept of identifying behaviors that make for success in certain tasks and occupations has found its way into many organizations that are looking for improved selection and development methods.

The industrial psychologist

The use of an industrial psychologist to test and interview both potential candidates for open positions and incumbent managers being considered for promotions is widespread in some organizations. Relying primarily on the structured interview technique, the industrial psychology approach is based on both traditional and contemporary theories of leadership. The conclusions drawn from these interviews are based on "self-assessment" criteria and patterns of response to specific questions that probe personality traits. Observations regarding the candidates' self-confidence, assertiveness, intelligence, loyalty, energy level, and so forth are typically included in a report that is prepared for senior management's attention. The following excerpt is representative of this kind of assessment:

> Mr. Nelson is a temperamental person who does not have a high frustration tolerance. He is overly sensitive and has a high need to be treated fairly. He is very critical of anything that constrains him from doing what he wants to do. He develops team friction by becoming too narrow in his analysis of situations.

> He is capable of being a very pleasant and personable individual but he has a tendency to be overly blunt, direct, and outspoken. He allows his emotions to have an adverse effect on his judgments. He is in the average range of intellectual ability when compared with other people in business and industry. He is a concrete and factual thinker. He is somewhat cautious but willing to take a risk. He participates within groups. He is an average listener. He has an average insight into understanding people. He can dominate others and can be autocratic. He can be forceful and demanding.

> His superior should encourage him to consider situations more broadly. He also needs to understand that sometimes it is necessary to encourage him not to become overly emotional.

The one-on-one structured assessment is based on the assumption that patterned responses to preselected questions are reliable predictors of behavior. This approach ignores the assumption that leadership occurs as part of a dynamic, interactive communication process. Leadership is influence. Influence cannot be self-assessed; it must be observed under conditions that require the person to perform in innovative, task, and maintenance roles.

The assessment center

In many companies the traditional methods of testing and interviewing have given way to an approach that is based on a series of simulation exercises. During these exercises the candidate undertakes tasks a leader would do while on the job. These simulations are conducted with observers documenting the behavior of the candidate. The recorded observations then serve as an evaluation of performance and a guide to selection and/or development. For a better understanding of how this process works, let's examine the basic steps one company followed in designing a leadership assessment program for middle management.

1. Through a series of interviews with senior and middle-level managers, a list of behavioral and operational leadership roles was established for assessment criteria. Figure 17 identifies and defines some of these criteria.

2. The criteria were then weighted by their relative importance to the job of a middle manager in each of the company's operating divisions. The weight of each criterion for one division is given in Figure 17.

3. Since the purpose of assessment can be for either selection or development (and in some instances for both) it was necessary to establish the derived outcome of the program. In this company it was determined that the assessment program should provide an objective data base for planning a companywide executive succession and development plan for each person participating in the program.

4. The format for the assessment program was then developed. A three-day program was designed wherein individuals participated in structured and unstructured group discussions, in-basket problems, speech and writing exercises, and problem-analysis simulations. These activities took the form of unassigned tasks, management games, questionnaires, situational encounters, and so on. As candidates completed the exercises, assessors recorded behaviors related to innovative, task, and maintenance management roles.

5. Participants were recommended by their immediate superiors for inclusion in the program. Final selections were made by the company's senior division management in accordance with corporate priorities and administrative considerations of participant groupings. Approximately 18 people participate each time the program is offered.

6. Experienced line and staff executives were combined to form a balanced staff of assessors. Assessors were selected from a variety of functions within the corporation to achieve the most appropriate mix of knowledge, professional skills, and job orientation. Assessors were selected from a level of management at least one level and preferably two levels higher than that of the participants. Both before and after the program, assessors met for training and evaluation. These training sessions were designed to establish uniformity among assessor ratings. Approximately nine assessors participated in each program.

7. After completion of the evaluative session, candidates were given feedback on their observed performance. Personal counseling was provided for each participant and a management development plan was drawn up with assistance from a professionally trained adviser. The evaluations were then reviewed with each manager's boss and subsequently became an integral part of the company's management succession and development plans.

Assessing leadership capabilities does not need to remain a perplexing or critical concern of top management. The years of research and practice devoted to leadership assessment have demon-

Figure 17. Sample leadership assessment criteria.

Weight	Criterion	Definition
10	Analytical skill	Effectiveness in seeking out pertinent data and defining the problem. Ability to reach logical conclusions based on the evidence at hand. Ability to make reasonable and reliable estimates of the time required to achieve objectives.
10	Interpersonal relationships	Ability to contribute to a cooperative work environment and develop and maintain a productive group effort and teamwork. Ability to utilize individual interests, needs, and abilities in order to achieve established objectives.
10	Administrative skills	Breadth and depth of business knowledge and personal capacity to utilize this knowledge in setting goals (objectives) and/or achieving established goals (objectives).
5	Emotional control	Ability to express feelings, perceptions, or points of view fairly and accurately. Willingness to trust the competence of others. Awareness of impact on other people. Ability to recognize and adapt to change. Ability to take action toward calculated risks based on sound judgment. Stability in performance under pressure and opposition. Ability to stay with a problem or line of thought until the matter is settled.
10	Work-oriented motivation	Broad range and diversity of interests oriented toward personal and organizational goals. Desire to participate in varied activities. Demonstration by actions that attainment of company objectives is as important as personal convenience. Ability to maintain a high level of activity.

5	Strategy management	Ability to develop the proper rationale for the allocation of corporate resources (capital, human, and systems) to ensure the attainment of both current and future performance objectives.
10	Capital resource management	Ability to predict, understand, and interpret the impact of decisions on changes in corporate financial statements.
5	Organization resource management	Ability to build and maintain the human organization from the standpoint of skill, structure, and spirit.
5	Systems resource management	Ability to understand and direct the flow of communications that integrate capital and human resources toward planned goals.
5	Constituency management	Ability to understand, fulfill, and/or mollify the expectations/needs of corporate publics such as shareholders, government, unions, public interest groups, private interest groups, and employees.
10	Innovation	Ability to think beyond the traditional or pedestrian. Ability to pursue new opportunities, better approaches, and better ways of doing things. Willingness to dream and possess a healthy dissatisfaction with the status quo. Appreciation for creativity.
15	Influence	Ability to influence all levels of the organization by virtue of actions, interpersonal relations, speech, and standards of conduct. Ability to inspire others to meet his or her high standards and expectations. Ability to motivate others to develop their own potential.

To determine the weight of each criterion, top management allocated 100 points across the total number of criteria. It gave more points to the items it considered most important, fewer points to the least important, and so on until points were all distributed according to relative importance.

strated that there are measurable behaviors that distinguish good leaders from poor ones. Twenty years of sustained research in such corporate settings as American Telephone and Telegraph, International Business Machines, General Electric, and Sears have been instrumental in making assessment techniques a viable and useful management tool.

Although a single approach to assessing leaders will not fit the needs of every organization, it appears safe to conclude that the characteristics of effective contemporary leadership remain constant from one organization to the next. Thus, the techniques of assessment might vary while the measurement criteria remain basically the same. The capability of assessing leaders, once a top-management luxury, is now an organizational necessity. The techniques available through the technology of organization behavior can assist management in making necessity a reality.

Assessing leaders is only part of the task, however. The question of how to develop tomorrow's leaders is perhaps one of the most important challenges that lie ahead for management. Are current approaches to developing leaders sufficient for the future or are radically different methods needed? This question serves as the subject of the next chapter.

NOTES

Early studies on leadership referred to in this chapter are:

Warren G. Bennis, "Leadership Theory and Administrative Behavior," *Administrative Science Quarterly*, December 1959.

Douglas McGregor, *The Human Side of Enterprise.* New York: McGraw-Hill, 1960.

R. M. Stogdill, "Personality Factors Associated with Leadership," *Journal of Psychology*, vol. 25, 1948.

E. B. Gowin, *The Executive and His Control of Men.* New York: Macmillan, 1915.

An excellent review of the findings of many early studies is provided by Cecil A. Gibb, "Leadership," in Gardner Lindzey (ed.), *Handbook of Social Psychology*, Vol. II. Reading, Mass.: Addison-Wesley, 1954.

Catherine Cox, *The Early Mental Traits of Three Hundred Geniuses.* Stanford, Calif.: Stanford University Press, 1926.

O. W. Caldwell and Beth L. Wellman, "Characteristics of School Leaders," *Journal of Educational Reseach,* vol. 14, 1926.

Chester I. Barnard, *The Functions of the Executive.* Cambridge, Mass.: Harvard University Press, 1962.

Irving Knickerbocker, "Leadership, A Conception and Some Implications," *Journal of Social Issues,* vol. 4, Spring 1948.

William A. Jenkins, "A Review of Leadership Studies with Particular Reference to Military Problems," *Psychology Bulletin,* vol. 44, 1947.

Robert McMurry, "The Case for Benevolent Autocracy," *Harvard Business Review,* January–February 1958.

11

Developing
contemporary managers

THE QUESTION of how to develop managers has remained a controversial issue in American business for many years. It is estimated that American industry spends more than $150 million annually on education and training aimed at improving the performance of supervisors and managers at all organizational levels. Although it is impossible to evaluate the overall impact this training has on corporate profitability, it is probably safe to assume that most organizations think of training as an end in itself rather than as a means to an end.

When asked why the company invests in a training function, the corporate executive is likely to respond with catchy phrases such as "to develop people for the future" or "to improve the company's human resources." However, when asked why the company has a research and development function this same executive's answer is likely to be more specific. He or she will reply, "to improve the company's competitive position in the marketplace" or "to increase profitability by introducing new and/or better products."

In short, the training and education functions are not perceived as a means of carrying out business plans, reaching goals, or improving efficiency and profitability in most corporations. In fact, many managers view these functions simply as "overhead" or necessary nuisances that must be tolerated in order to appease employees.

Many professional management development specialists recognize management's casual regard for their function, so they conduct a constant search for new approaches or techniques—a kind of surefire training method—that will convince executive management once and for all of their value to the organization. With this quest has come a basketful of fads ranging from off-the-shelf problem-solving courses, to sensitivity training, to the latest fad—behavior modification.

Behind the search for surefire answers on how to develop managers are some basic answers on how to develop managers to manage the contemporary workforce. The answers do not rest with a single approach to management development. Rather, they can be found through an examination of the relationship between managerial values and the management development process itself. The contrast between the contemporary and traditional manager provides a useful frame of reference for considering some of the underlying principles that determine the effectiveness of a development process. These principles are not intended as statements of law concerning human behavior, but they have become commonly accepted guidelines shared by organization behavior practitioners.

Principle 1. Management Development Is a Line Responsibility

Management development is, in its purest form, managers developing managers. Classroom training, reading, and other forms of awareness can contribute significantly to the process, but the most potent form of development occurs on the job itself. The behavior of the boss, the content of the job, the working environment, the norms of the work unit, and the management style set at the top of the organization all play a vital role in the management development process.

The traditional view of management development is that it is a staff responsibility. Managers with profit-and-loss responsibility tended to rely on staff specialists to develop their subordinates while they took care of "running the business." The contemporary manager, however, recognizes that management development is an integral part of the business and accepts responsibility for results in this area just as he or she would accept responsibility for sales, productivity, or earnings.

Managers with a contemporary value orientation are more likely to accept responsibility for developing subordinates than managers with traditional values. More specifically, managers who score high on the locus-of-control dimension are more likely to coach and guide their subordinates' development than those with low scores. They are more likely to see to it that plans for development are carried out and they are not reluctant to provide feedback and report on progress.

Principle 2. Management Development Is Influenced Most by the Immediate Supervisor

For a recent survey that asked how well-managed organizations develop their managers and executives, Lester A. Digman studied several major corporations known for their excellence in management development. He concluded that, without exception, these companies "work on the premise that the vast majority of actual development occurs on the job through the handling of progressively more responsible assignments and problems under fire."* The study also concluded that the "predominant feeling is that development on the job is greatly enhanced by coaching from the individual's immediate manager, where the employee is taught

* Dale Yoder and Herbert G. Henemon, Jr., eds., *Training and Development: ASPA Handbook of Personnel and Industrial Relations* (Washington, D.C.: The Bureau of National Affairs, 1977).

to handle his or her job through guided experience, in a kind of student/teacher relationship."

The interaction between the employee and the manager is *the* vital ingredient in the development process. The values held by the manager will, therefore, significantly influence the kind of management development that results. Conflicts between employee values and managerial values can impede the development process. Where values are shared, the development process is enriched.

To the employee, the superior represents the organization's formal authority. It is the superior who selects the employee's assignments and opportunities to learn on the job. The superior's practices, attitudes, and style are observed and either emulated or rejected by the subordinate. Managers scoring high on the self-esteem dimension tend to have a greater capacity for developing employees than managers with low self-esteem.

Principle 3. Management Development Is Self-Development

Management development does not begin from a zero base. Each person brings a unique set of abilities, aspirations, motivations, and values to the job. These characteristics have the potential of becoming a tremendous resource to management development. Conversely, these same characteristics can impede the development process.

A person's orientation toward risk taking in development is a function of his or her dependency value orientation. Tolerance of ambiguity or need for reassurance can affect the choice of professional disciplines. In short, personal values influence motivation to develop in a specific direction. People who score high on the tolerance-for-ambiguity and self-esteem dimensions tend to have a greater awareness of their own development needs and are more likely to experiment with different approaches to self-development than their counterparts with lower scores.

Principle 4. Management Development Needs to Be Individually Tailored

A development plan must accommodate each person's values and unique learning abilities. Too often, the tendency to prescribe universal approaches and solutions has made development a confusing and overly generalized process. Although this notion does not preclude a coordinated company program or group development methods, it does suggest that a single lock-step program that creates identical experiences for all managers is not the best approach. There is no one best way to develop managers.

A formal management development program can be extremely useful in raising the general level of competency in a given area. It is important, however, to be able to differentiate whether the competency problem is attributable to a lack of knowledge, skill, or performance or to a value orientation. A second approach to management development begins with an individual assessment of these factors.

People with high self-esteem scores are more likely to conduct a personal inventory of these factors than those with low scores. Furthermore, their receptivity to self-improvement objectives is greater than it is for those with low self-esteem scores.

Principle 5. Management Development Requires Action(s)

Management development requires behavioral change. Change is caused by the individual and comes about because of a person's perception and response to events and stimuli. Management development is a personal rather than a mechanistic process. Development occurs because people choose to act or respond. Often the response or action is not overt, since new thoughts or attitudes may be weighed or tested in covert ways. Assimilating and integrating new knowledge, skills, and behaviors are all development processes.

Before development occurs, it might be necessary to change a value orientation. Creating an awareness of the link between values and development is an important step in getting people to act in new or different ways. Those with high tolerance-of-ambiguity and locus-of-control scores tend to identify and change the values that ultimately lead to changes in awareness, skill, or behavior.

Principle 6. Management Development Is Aided by Controls

Like all management activities, management development needs to be controlled. Managers learn more effectively and systematically if they understand the learning objectives, the skills they are expected to master, and the behaviors they are expected to manifest.

People whose value orientation measures high on the locus-of-control dimension are more likely to establish standards and benchmarks for personal development than people who score low on this dimension. Because they believe that advancement depends on achievement rather than political affiliation, those who score high on locus of control are likely to be more responsive to performance reviews and are more highly motivated to establish personal controls for managing their development than those with low scores.

Principle 7. Management Development Is Influenced by Organization Climate

The climate of the organization can either facilitate or impede the achievement of desired management development objectives. The ideal organization climate for management development is one that encourages and supports innovation, examination of existing management practices, and experimentation with new behavior. In this climate, managers can develop creative ways of solving new or recurring problems, adopt challenging standards of excellence, and try newly developed techniques. Managers with high scores on social judgment tend to be more adept at creating this type of environment than those with low scores. Furthermore, those who score low on the need-for-dependency dimension are more likely to support innovation than risk-adverse managers who score high on this dimension.

Principle 8. Management Development Is a Continuous Process

Management development is an ongoing process. Periodic reassessment and recycling of development in light of new organizational requirements and/or new managerial demands are necessary. Management development, therefore, often occurs in unstructured, spontaneous situations.

Those who value structure highly, who have low scores on the tolerance-of-ambiguity dimension, are likely to experience discomfort with frequent development and continuous behavioral adjustment. Those who value an unstructured environment will tend to have a greater capacity to accept the notion that development, once initiated, never ends.

Summary

As organizations continue to orchestrate their growth, it becomes increasingly important for them to develop the capability to inventory their managerial style. Organizations must have managers with the capacity to create an environment that encourages innovative management development. And these managers must take innovative approaches to motivate the contemporary employee. Management value orientations must be measured and, where necessary, altered to respond to the changing demands of the workforce. Organizations will have to begin with an examination of the values both of managers and of their employees—possible future managers. This examination must become an integral part of managing the business. Organization planners must continue to consider such factors as experience, skill, education, and performance, but they must also develop the capability of achieving the proper ratio of contemporary managers to contemporary employees.

The emergence of the contemporary employee has placed a demand on organizations to professionalize their management development efforts. In the future, other organizational and management practices will have to change to respond to the value orientation of the new workforce. These changes are the subject of the next chapter.

12

Surveying employee attitudes

IN RECENT YEARS, many companies have been experimenting with various methods of collecting information dealing with day-to-day and long-range employer/employee relations problems that affect corporate profitability. The emergence of the contemporary workforce has placed an additional demand on management. This workforce wants to be heard and to be part of the company's decision-making process. However, with the increased complexity of running the day-to-day affairs of a business, it is not uncommon for management to be unaware of what employees are thinking, what actions they might be contemplating, or what their feelings are on any number of important organizational considerations such as compensation, job satisfaction, management practices, promotional opportunities, and productivity.

In one typical case, a newly appointed top-management representative was greatly disturbed when he observed the steadily rising costs in his division with little or no increase in productivity. His concern became even greater as he heard numerous complaints from employees regarding such matters as work hours, limited opportunities for advancement, and dissatisfaction with pay and benefits. To explore the problems, he requested an in-depth survey of these employee concerns.

Why Survey Attitudes?

This executive, like many others, recognized that surveying employee attitudes can serve the basic purpose of providing management with an evaluation of the actual or potential effectiveness of the organization. Monitoring changes in employee attitudes can lead to improved communications between employees and management. However, upward communication can be a major problem in any organization. Most employees are hesitant to risk the consequences of communicating negative information to their superiors. Even when problems are expressed, rarely do they filter through the many layers of management to the top of the hierarchy. Management decisions are often made without adequate knowledge about the attitudes and behavior of employees.

To address the problems related to upward communication, many organizations have expended a great deal of time and effort developing means for getting input from the lower echelons. These means range from the highly informal suggestion box to formalized employee/management meetings. Although information obtained through these methods is often valuable, it is also incomplete. A lack of in-depth probing, consistent formats, guaranteed employee anonymity, and strong statistical analyses results in inadequate data that usually do not even penetrate the top decision-making levels in the organization. It is not enough simply to ask employees about their feelings or even to rely on the organization's "lieutenants." Rather, to determine the state of employee attitudes properly, it is necessary to utilize the newly developed behavioral science principles and methods for surveying employee attitudes.

In addition to providing management with an analysis of the overall morale of the organization, surveying the attitudes of employees can be an important first step in improving the performance of the organization. To illustrate this point, let's examine Pillsbury's experience with employee surveys.*

* The information in this section came from Louis I. Gelfand, "Communicate Through Your Supervisors," *Harvard Business Review*, November–December, 1970.

The managers of the seven Pillsbury flour mills, when asked in late 1966 what in their operation most needed improvement, listed "relationship deterioration" as the major problem. An examination of internal communications followed, including surveys of 500 hourly (unionized) employees at the flour mills, grocery products plants, and refrigerated foods plants. Also, mail questionnaires were sent to 100 field sales employees.

The study underscored that good communications and favorable employee attitudes go hand in hand. A plant in which the manager emphasized communication in his weekly planning sessions and held supervisory personnel accountable for it rated highest: Some 81 percent of the personnel indicated that the company "tries to give employees a fair deal." In a plant in which communication was considered poor, 34 percent said the company tried to keep them informed, and 56 percent said the company tried to give them "a fair deal."

Headquarters employees knew what was going on, but plant employees expressed special interest in the speed of communication and in knowing more about job security, company plans, growth of production, manpower development, and research in new products. They wanted to get information from their supervisors; too much of it was coming through the grapevine.

After Robert J. Keith, then president, held a conference to discuss the survey findings with top management, a pilot project was begun to improve internal communications at the Ogden, Utah, flour mill. This mill had about 70 union employees and 30 salaried persons. Also, the company's monthly magazine was changed to a tabloid in order to speed up the dispersal of information and, because of its larger size, to permit detail.

The pilot project was expanded to all 17 plants. A simple format included (1) setting aside about 15 minutes of the workday every week, during which each supervisor met with his or her group; (2) taking a few minutes to report verbally to the group on matters that might interest them; and (3) using the balance of the time for questions and answers to learn what was on the minds of the employees. Questions that could not be answered were deferred until the next meeting.

The plan was designed to provide both the "whats" and the "whys" behind the "whats." Implementation of the plan in the various plants was not forced; rather, it was enlisted under a "home rule" principle.

Once it was decided to implement the program, meetings to discuss it were held with department heads. Plant managers met with supervisors to discuss questions that might arise—questions relating to production data, new products, capital expenditures and their rationale, customer information, product information, reasons for processes and procedures, and so on. The ground rules were to avoid company propaganda, avoid labor relations matters and negotiable items, provide information, seek help to solve problems, and be willing to acknowledge mistakes.

The response to the program was positive. In one plant, after 18 months with the program, 114 employees said they liked the program; only 17 did not. Asked if they knew more about the company than before, 105 answered "yes" and 14 said "no."

Grievances were reduced. Twenty-five percent of the ideas generated in the program were considered of practical value. In one 700-employee installation, the manager declined to implement the program because he said his people knew what was going on. Some 18 months later he resigned. His successor installed the program on the first day of his new assignment. He reported that "We had hundreds of questions, nearly 500 the first couple of weeks. The people were hungry for information. Now we get about 60 to 70 questions a week."

As this experience shows, attitudes are related to organization performance (behavior). When dealing with attitudes, we are concerned more with predispositions to behave (intents). The stronger the attitudes, the stronger the intent. The stronger the intent, the more likely behavior will follow. When there is strong evidence of employee dissatisfaction, as there was in the Pillsbury example, this dissatisfaction usually affects some element(s) of employee performance. Figure 18 illustrates this relationship.

Conducting employee attitude surveys, then, provides management with the opportunity to assess the overall psychological climate within the workforce. By obtaining information on employee attitudes toward specific company policies, practices, programs, and a range of other categories, management can pinpoint problems within particular employee groups such as departments or job

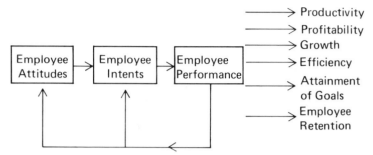

Figure 18. Relationship of attitudes to performance.

families. Then by developing appropriate plans of action to address these problems, as in the Pillsbury case, management can eliminate factors that hinder effective employee performance.

Employee attitude surveys also serve as a form of therapy for those who participate in the survey process. Surveys allow employees to express their opinions to management freely in an open or anonymous way. Becoming involved in the total process of sharing information, receiving feedback from management on other employees' views, and then participating in planning sessions aimed at organizational improvements, employees are made to feel that they are a vital factor in the organization's decision-making process.

In short, surveying employee attitudes can provide an information base that can assist management and employees with improving organization performance. Without a regular monitoring mechanism for taking the temperature and pulse of the organization, management runs the risk of ignoring important information about its major asset—people.

What to Survey

Surveys can be used for a number of different organizational purposes. Sometimes they allow an organization to compare changes in its general climate over a period of time. Other times, they are used to determine where potential employee problems are located. Typically, they are administered as an after-the-fact reaction to such problems as large turnover, absenteeism, low productivity, declining morale, or unionization attempts. Regardless of the purpose, sampling employee attitudes is not unlike taking the organization's pulse, monitoring its heartbeat, and checking its blood pressure. Surveying employee attitudes can be applied to a number of important management concerns.

Organization climate survey

Many times an organization wants to "keep in touch" with the morale of employees and to do so as discreetly as possible, without utilizing in-depth survey methods. One example of such a method is the organization climate survey that can be used to assess and prioritize selected factors related to the mood of the people in the organization.

This survey is designed to achieve what the Roper and Gallup polls achieve: an overall analysis of current attitudes and attitude trends. One organization, for example, administers this survey three or four times a year to a small, scientifically selected sample of employees in order to monitor the overall morale of its employees. Much like a periodic physical checkup, this survey acts as a preventive measure in that it identifies morale problems before they become "malignant" or "inoperable." The climate index has proved useful to this company's management by identifying and measuring attitude trends in the organization and by providing comparisons of attitude changes over time.

Organization performance survey

Whereas an organization climate survey is intended to measure the overall morale of the organization, an organization performance survey serves the purpose of providing management with an in-depth measurement of employee attitudes on different aspects of their jobs, their departments, company programs, and so forth.

An organization performance survey typically focuses on employee attitudes toward productivity, teamwork, compensation, job security, and a number of other factors related to employees' attitudes concerning the performance of the company. The president of a mid-sized electronics firm decided to assess the attitudes of his entire organization, which had over 4,000 employees. The results of the survey (which measured 17 organizational dimensions) indicated that employees were most concerned with their level of compensation, the lack of promotional opportunities in the company, and the lack of management's responsiveness to their ideas and problems. Employees also indicated that under more optimal organizational conditions, their own productivity could be improved significantly. Table 5 lists the dimensions by rank. Specific items within these dimensions were also rank-ordered, enabling management to identify the specific nature of each problem area.

Results of the survey were fed back to management two weeks after it was made. The results were presented to small groups, and discussions were held with all employees who participated in the survey.

Since one of the major findings of the survey was that employees did not feel they had enough input into those decisions that ultimately affected them, management decided to involve them in the process of developing recommendations based on the results of the survey. The company's president realized the advantages of having such input in that employees often have excellent ideas about how to improve their own satisfaction and motivation. By becoming part of the survey process, employees became much more committed to ensuring that any and all actions taken would be effective.

The final product of this survey process was a well-defined action plan for solving the problems identified by employees. The reasons for inaction on some problems—because, for example, the solutions would be contrary to corporate policy or cost more than any realized benefits—were explained. By implementing the necessary corrective actions and adjustments and by restoring faith in

Table 5. Dimensions rank-ordered in terms of overall need for change.

Rank	Dimension
1	Compensation
2	Promotion opportunities
3	Responsiveness to employees
4	Productivity
5	Training and education
6	Participative decision making
7	Concern for employees
8	Downward communication
9	Performance standards
10	Teamwork
11	Internal job satisfaction
12	Structure
13	External job satisfaction
14	Loyalty to company
15	Interpersonal climate
16	Job security
17	Employee benefits

management, it was possible for the company to achieve major gains in employee productivity.

Because it had made the organization performance survey and followed up with group discussions, employees recognized that management was interested in their concerns. The correction of their real/perceived problems restored credibility to the company's contention that its most valued resource was its employees.

Safety audit

Safety is of major concern to most organizations. This concern stems from an implicit concern for the employees' welfare as well as the cost to the organization in terms of workers' compensation and lost-time accidents. Although most organizations will readily admit that the single most likely cause of accidents is organizational and individual attitudes, few use current behavioral methods to help stem such accidents.

A safety audit is one method for determining employee attitudes toward safety and acting upon results to reduce the number and severity of accidents. A manufacturing department of an organization with a high incidence of lost time due to accidents began surveying its employees to measure their attitudes toward safety. The survey also encouraged employees to recommend actions for improving safety conditions in their work environments. By involving employees and management in the audit procedure, management obtained greater employee commitment to reducing accidents. These efforts substantially reduced the number of accidents, improved downtime losses, and saved the company major expense in workers' compensation claims.

Communications audit

Most organizations attempt to determine the effectiveness of internal communications. Unfortunately, however, they limit their measurement of effectiveness to their in-house publications. Rarely do they attempt to measure both formal and informal communications. A communications audit can be used to give priority to the degree and location of communication problems that might affect the performance of employees. An audit should examine employee perceptions of the accuracy, importance, timeliness, and quantity of information received from various communication sources—supervisors, management, fellow employees, the grapevine, and the company's printed media.

Figure 19 illustrates one of the reports used to convey the results of a communications audit that was administered to an organization experiencing difficulties with communications between management and employees. The audit made it possible to analyze the organization's formal and informal communications by identifying the quantity and quality of communication in the company. By focusing its attention on the specific communication

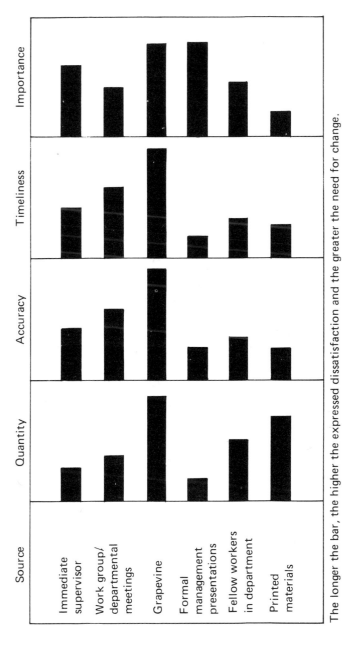

The longer the bar, the higher the expressed dissatisfaction and the greater the need for change.

Figure 19. Comparison of six organizational sources of information.

source problems the management of this company was able to identify the precise nature and location of its communication problems. Acting on its findings resulted in an overall improvement in communications between management and employees, as measured by a similar survey administered one year later. An understanding of the effectiveness of communications within an organization can often be a key to improving relationships between management and employees. A communications audit helps provide management with the capability to assess the strengths and limitations of the organization's ongoing efforts.

How to Measure Attitudes

The traditional approach to measuring employee attitudes might be described as follows. An internal employee, usually with little or no background in contemporary behavioral science methodology, develops an attitude survey at the request of a manager to find out how employees feel about some aspect or aspects of their work environment. The survey typically elicits either yes or no responses or asks employees to answer each question on some form of a numerical scale. When the survey has been administered, results are analyzed (often over a period of two or three months) and explained to the manager. Change may or may not result from this survey, but regardless of the outcomes, the employee never hears about it again.

For descriptive purposes, it would be useful to dissect this traditional process further. It was stated that an internal employee develops an attitude survey. In many cases, this employee has little or no background in contemporary behavioral science methods. The survey may look interesting, but it is often poorly developed. Even if action is taken on the survey results, it often has a negative rather than a positive impact because of the superficiality of the information upon which it is based.

To counter this problem, many organizations have gone to the opposite extreme. They have developed survey approaches that are highly sophisticated but so complex that managers in the organization cannot interpret the data. Instead, they receive reports that look more like tables in a dissertation for a doctoral degree than simple results reflecting the feelings of their employees. Inevitably, no action is taken on these results.

It was also stated that the traditional attitude survey approach is used to "find out how employees feel about some aspect or aspects of their work environment," focusing only on employee attitudes. If management is concerned with how to motivate employees for increased performance, knowledge of their present attitudes does *not* provide enough information. Improving attitudes does not necessarily result in improved performance. It is important to gather more information about employees than the degree of their satisfaction with the work environment.

The typical attitude survey process is characterized by analyzing results over a two- or three-month period. Such turnaround time is much too long. Survey results reflect information about employees at the time of administration. Two or three months later, employees may feel quite differently.

It was suggested that "change may or may not result from the survey, but regardless of the outcomes, the employee never hears about it again." To survey employees without feeding back results can be a fatal mistake. Why? First, because it is the employees who must make any change work. If they are left out of the process, they will not encourage change and may even work against it. Second, if employees do not see change resulting from the attitude survey process, they will tend not to support further attempts to solicit their input. Too many organizations fail with their attitude survey approach because they do not draw a clear link between survey results and the changes occurring. Finally, surveys are often designed to reflect only management's concern about the organization (factors such as productivity, loyalty to company, and personal performance). Asking the staff specialist to design a survey for management's use is a critical mistake. Rather, surveys should reflect the concerns of both management and employees.

Figure 20. Need-for-change survey items.

---

00. MANAGEMENT DOES NOT USUALLY TOLERATE POOR PERFORMANCE.

a. Presently?	Strongly Disagree	1	2	3	4	5	6	7	Strongly Agree
b. Ideally?	Strongly Disagree	1	2	3	4	5	6	7	Strongly Agree
c. Importance?	Unimportant	1	2	3	4	5	6	7	Important

The need-for-change index

The application of contemporary behavioral science methodologies to the attitude survey process greatly enhances successful change in the performance of employees. In response to the traditional problems associated with the attitude survey process, alternative methods are now being used by a number of major corporations to survey employee attitudes on a number of organizational concerns.

The new approach requires that surveys provide more information to managers than simple answers about employee feelings. Employee performance is a function of both the feelings and intents (expectancy) of the employee. Therefore, a basic element of the new approach developed by Mark G. Mindell and myself utilizes what we refer to as a Need-for-Change Index. This index provides management with a rank ordering (or prioritizing) of employee attitudes and intents. When respondents evaluate survey items, they are asked to indicate.

1. How they presently view the condition (feelings).
2. How they would prefer the condition under more ideal circumstances (intent).
3. How important the condition is to them.

By taking the difference between their evaluation of No. 1 and No. 2 and multiplying this difference by their evaluation of No. 3, a need-for-change score is calculated. Figure 20 gives an example item from one of the surveys that utilizes this index.

Figure 21. Items in the job security dimension rank-ordered in terms of need for change.

RANK (Need for Change)

1   How do you rate this company in providing job secu-
     rity for people like yourself?

2   My job is an important part of this company.

3   I expect to be working at this company for at least five
     more years.

The need-for-change score provides management and employees with reports that can be easily understood. For example, in one particular department, the dimension of job security received the highest overall need-for-change score. Already the manager knows that of all employee concerns, job security is the greatest source of discontent. By examining the report further, the manager can determine quickly and precisely where the concerns rest (see Figure 21).

The number used to calculate the need-for-change score indicates the discrepancy between present conditions and intended or expected conditions. When accounting for importance (weighting), the higher the number, the greater the need for improving satisfaction with that item.

The Need-for-Change Index, then, can be used to establish priorities on employee concerns for management action. When measuring employee attitudes it is not enough to ask questions that elicit a yes or no response. Nor is it advisable to place each question on a scale of one to five, one to seven, or within any other numerical range. Attitudes are formed from past experience. We learn to evaluate objects, people, and events in terms of good/bad, like/dislike, favorable/unfavorable, and so forth. Attitudes are learned. The first day an employee takes a job, he or she begins to form attitudes about the job. These attitudes, good or bad, will eventually lead to some form of behavior that affects corporate profitability, either directly or indirectly. Since attitudes can be measured, there is no reason for an organization to rely upon speculation or "intuitive" feelings about employee attitudes. To make reliable measures of attitudes, it is necessary to know more than a person's present feelings; we must know his or her intent to act on those feelings. The Need-for-Change Index provides this form of measurement.

How to Manage the Survey Process

Surveys should not simply be administered, analyzed, and then forgotten. Properly used, they can be a powerful technique for bringing about organizational improvements. However, most surveys are not used properly. At best, they provide top management with data for changing policies and/or procedures. At worst, they have been placed in the files of the company research department and left to gather dust.

The process of surveying employees should be regarded much like a financial audit. Just as the company's financial condition must be reviewed regularly, so, too, must employee/management relationships be audited. For surveys to be conducted in a professional manner, they should follow these management guidelines:

Begin with an orientation to act on survey results. The key factor in the success or failure of any survey is the commitment management makes to act on the results. The process of administering a survey inevitably raises expectations on the part of employees that some action will be taken. Collecting information from employees should be considered part of a broader action plan to bring about needed organizational changes. It is important for management to be involved in the preliminary planning of the survey process.

Use only a survey that has proven reliability and validity and that displays results in an easily understood format. Before committing the company to undertaking a survey, management should clearly understand the format for reporting results. Surveys that use too many numbers and tables should be avoided. On the other hand, management should be aware of oversimplistic surveys that report only percentages without accounting for factors such as the importance of employee concerns. To utilize the data from a survey effectively, management should be presented with a priority list of employee concerns and the reasons for these concerns.

See that the survey is designed to measure dimensions of concern to both management and employees. The survey should be designed in such a way that it has the potential of surfacing latent issues and problems at both the management and the employee level. If the questions on the survey are not important to employees, their interest in the process will be minimal. It is often helpful to conduct preliminary interviews with a cross section of employees to help frame the questions and to narrow the survey to the most relevant issues.

See that information about the survey is made public. Once a determination has been made as to who will participate in the survey, it is important to disseminate information regarding the purpose, scope, and ultimate use of the survey information. Communications about the survey should specify who will participate in the survey (entire population, random sample, or other grouping), who will review survey results, and how the results will be fed back to employees.

See that the survey examines both the current state of attitudes and the intended (expected) behavioral state. Without a proper statistical design, a survey can produce information that might suggest a problem that is not really important to employees. For example, employees might express a high degree of dissatisfaction with the company's parking situation, but in relative terms, this problem may not be as important as many other concerns they have. For management to focus its attention on the most important problems, the design of the survey must account for current and expected conditions, weighted by some measure of importance.

Provide feedback to employees. If there is a single piece of accepted wisdom about surveying employees it is this: To ensure that the survey process has a positive impact on the overall morale of employees, they should receive feedback on the results of the survey soon after they have completed it. Yet in a 1975 survey of "Human Resource Practices," Hay Associates found that only 63 percent of the organizations that conduct surveys communicate the results to the participants and 23 percent communicate the results only to senior management. These figures represent a substantial increase over a National Conference Board study in 1951 that found only 23 percent of the companies communicating survey results to employees, but they also indicate that many organizations ignore the important benefit that can be realized by including employees in the total survey process.

Involve management in the feedback and action-planning processes. Studies conducted at the Institute for Social Research at the University of Michigan and published in 1972 indicate that if surveys are to be successful, management must participate in the total process—planning at the initial stages, feedback of results to employees, and planning and implementing of changes that result from the survey information. The feedback and action-planning steps can be taken by conducting feedback sessions with the top-executive team (at the appropriate organizational level) and then moving these sessions down through the hierarchy. Each manager should preside at a meeting with his subordinates at which the data are discussed. Subordinates should be asked to help interpret the data. Plans should be designed to facilitate making constructive changes and for initiating the introduction of the data at the next lower level.

See that management action plans are linked to the survey results. In many instances survey data are collected, reported to top management, and then briefly summarized in group meetings or the company newsletter. Although organizational changes often do take place as a result of the information collected in the survey, management may not draw an association between employee concerns and management action. The following memorandum illustrates how actions should be tied to survey results:

April 18, 1979

MEMORANDUM TO: All Company Employees

FROM: Richard J. Harris, President

SUBJECT: Attitude Survey

You have just completed an attitude survey and your message has come through loud and clear. You want to know more about the company goals, plans, and policies and how they affect you.

Specifically, you want to know more about policies for hiring, promotions, performance evaluation, job posting procedures, merit increases. You want to know more about policy relating to compensation and benefits programs. You want better channels of communication among all groups—managers, supervisors, and employees. You want a stronger, more consistent effort made for training and individual development programs.

We are beginning at once to address these issues more vigorously than we have in the past. There is much work to be done and some of these changes will take time to implement fully. From all of you we need help, cooperation, ideas, and comments so that we can really do the job right. Much of the groundwork for evaluating and formulating policies will come from discussion groups and meetings at all levels. How well we do depends in large part on what we all put into it.

From now on there will be quarterly meetings with all employees. These will run from one to two hours and will be held in one of the cafeterias. Because of space limitations there will be several groups, but all meetings will be held on the same day. These will cover:

1. How we did for the last quarter—how many presses were shipped, how many new orders were booked, how much money we made

2. How we are doing in the marketplace, how we stack up against the competition, what we are doing to maintain or improve our competitive position, what we forecast for the near term, how we are allocating our resources, financial and otherwise, what problems we have, and what we are doing to solve them.

3. How we are doing on the various programs of particular interest to each of us, including compensation and benefits surveys and training and individual development programs, and on other appropriate personnel policy matters.

4. A question-and-answer period, in which everyone will be encouraged to speak up on those things that are of real concern. Those questions that can be answered at the meeting will be. Those that can't will be answered as soon as possible after the meeting.

Our first quarterly meeting will be held on Friday, May 11, 1979. By then, we will have the financial results of the year ending March 31, 1979. If you have any questions or comments you think would be of interest to bring up, send them to the personnel department not later than May 2, 1979.

Future meetings will be held approximately five (5) weeks after the end of every quarter. This is to allow the accounting department time to close the books and prepare material.

Next year at this time we will take another attitude survey. I expect it to show that the questions and concerns you have today will have been addressed in a thoughtful and professional way, and that the company has moved from a very good place to work to the best place to work.

Richard J. Harris
President

RJH/pab

For many organization members, the completion of an attitude survey is the first exposure they have to an organizational improvement effort. The administration of an attitude survey presents an opportunity for active participation in the process of bringing about productivity and quality of work life improvements. If done properly, an employee attitude survey can serve the basic purpose identified earlier in this chapter; namely, to provide management with an evaluation of the actual or potential effectiveness of the organization's human resource.

Summary

Why should the question of surveying employee attitudes be included in a book that focuses on improving organizational profitability? What does surveying accomplish? Surveying provides management with an organized method of obtaining information from employees. This information can then be used as a first step toward bringing about improvements in employee performance and organizational conditions that affect performance.

Surveys can be used to assess the overall climate of the organization, to give management an indication of the company's general health. They can also be used to measure the relative success of company policies, practices, and programs, including such concerns as safety and communications. The measurement of attitudes, however, should follow good organization behavior practices. The Need-for-Change Index enables management to use the information provided by the various forms of employee surveys in an effective manner.

The survey process should follow some important guidelines. First, management should be sure that the survey used is scientifically sound but still simple enough for managers to understand and act upon the results. Second, surveys should yield results that clearly suggest methods for motivating employees better. Examining feelings alone is not enough; rather, surveys must examine key areas that are linked directly to employee performance. Third, the results of the survey should be fed back to managers and employees. Fourth, the results should be acted upon. Last, management actions should be linked directly to the concerns of employees as they were presented in the survey.

Before a survey is administered, management should be committed to improving organizational conditions. As specific actions are applied to the organization, surveyed employees must be made aware of the link between the survey process and the resultant actions. Only after such a link is clearly communicated can the success of future attempts to solicit the view of employees be ensured.

To implement changes that result from the survey process successfully, it is often necessary to move employees from a concern for their individual welfares to a concern for the welfare of their work unit. To accomplish this, it is often necessary to introduce concepts and management practices that focus employees on team performance—the subject of the next chapter.

13

Developing teamwork in today's environment

IN SPITE of the current fashionableness of the word "team" and its apparent relevance to organizations, many executives are asking how to improve teamwork from the workforce and get increased profitability. But what does the label "team" mean to people who use it to characterize the behavior of individuals who comprise a group? An obvious carryover from the world of sports, the team metaphor implies that the skill and knowledge of each group member will be utilized to the maximum extent. The label is often used in organizations when we want to convey a sense of unity, commonality, and camaraderie, or a spirit of oneness.

Usually, a team consists of any organizational unit whose members report to the same superior in the structural hierarchy. It may also be made up of members from several levels who work under the direction of a superior or an assigned leader. Teams may be temporary work units such as project teams or task forces. On a much larger, more permanent scale, the organization itself may be considered a team in that organization grows out of a desire on the part of a collection of people to achieve certain objectives that cannot be obtained from individual effort. In most organizational hierarchies there are multiple teams that can function vertically, diagonally, or horizontally.

Probably because the term is fashionable and apparently relevant to organizations, many managers refer to the work unit for which they are responsible as a team long before it lives up to that connotation. To be called a team might have a certain psychic unifying power, but it is unwise for management to assume that its many divisions and departments are teamlike in behavior or work output.

How, then, can managers develop and sustain an effective team? The answer to this question, provided by behavioral science literature, is often so complex or intricate in its detail that managers are left with the feeling that managing a team requires a deep understanding of the psychosocial principles of human behavior. Although there is no definite formula for managers to follow, there are some basic behavioral principles that, if understood at a conceptual level, can help those in leadership roles formulate their own strategies and actions for increasing profitability through teams.

Building Teamwork Around Tasks

To understand how to establish and sustain teamwork, it is essential to examine the meaning and purpose of teams as they function in an organizational setting. Teams are usually formed and developed along one of two different tracks that William I. Gordon and I have labeled the "task track" and the "relationship track."* Let us consider the phases through which an organization usually progresses if it follows a task track by examining the George Hantscho story as told by the son of the company's founder.

THE HANTSCHO COMPANY

The Hantscho story began with my father, who was a strong person in almost all respects. He grew up in the eastern part of old Germany

---

* William I. Gordon and Roger J. Howe, *Team Dynamics in Developing Organizations* (Dubuque, Iowa: Kendall Hunt, 1977).

near the Czechoslovakian border and learned his trade in the schools still popular in Germany today. He left home at an early age to get away from family and the post-World War I chaos in Germany. After several years in the merchant marine he eventually landed in the United States in the late 1920s. By the mid-1930s he was working for a printing machinery manufacturer in Mt. Vernon, New York, and thereby began a lifelong association with that industry. He left this company in 1951 after working his way up in the organization to division manager.

In 1952 he founded the Graphic Arts Machine Company in Mt. Vernon, bought several used machine tools, designed a new style of machine, and started business. The key ingredients, I believe, in his philosophy of business were an absolute dedication to fulfillment of customer obligations and total loyalty of his staff.

His management style was totally informal, without a vestige of directed business systems planning. He booked the orders based on his perception of what he felt the company could do and then simply depended on his people to fulfill that customer obligation. Knowing my father's nature (you crossed him only once), compliments from him were a friendly word, a raise, or both. His staff generally moved mountains to overcome obstacles and meet a predetermined shipping date.

In a sense, my father's method of management was to hire fully competent people, tell them what he wanted, and leave them alone to figure out how to do it. While always available to answer questions, make decisions, and/or offer advice, he was not prone to involving himself in an orderly way in the day-to-day operation. Through his behavior, he made it quite clear that although he was the ultimate decision maker his department managers had the responsibility and authority to make whatever decisions were necessary to build a high-quality product in a timely, efficient manner.

The business prospered into the late 1950s and early 1960s, but it soon became so large that the lack of formal systems began to be a problem. Newer employees who did not have the long-term association with my father and the resulting deep, almost blind, faith in the man began to mill around and look for leadership and a more tangible commitment from the company about their future. A union fight developed. It was defeated, but it left my father somewhat disillusioned, and changes in the company began to take place.

By the mid-1960s the business had grown considerably and was developing serious scheduling and cost control problems. It had also developed a very strong market reputation and was staffed largely by European-trained people. Supervisors were generally advanced based on their technical skills rather than their supervisory skills. Supervisory failings generally were dealt with by transfer back to a lesser job and the advancement of another skilled person who could handle supervisory duties better.

The paternalistic style of my father gradually changed to what I'll call "enlightened human relations." The introduction of rate ranges, merit review programs, and employee surveys were evidence of his concern for "humanizing" his approach to management. The effects of these changes in management style were clearer organizational responsibilities and more tangible delegation of authority—in short, a more formal management system. The key element that was preserved as the company continued to grow was the strong commitment to customer obligations, feedback from sales and service as the major input to product development, and strict adherence to task accomplishment. Customer complaints were regularly fed directly to the company's senior management.

There is no question in my mind that throughout the growth of the company the fundamental ingredients of success never changed; namely, (1) a good, up-to-date, quality product, (2) a constant focus of attention on fulfilling customer obligations, and (3) a constructive work environment, uncluttered with outside influences, wherein qualified people could provide (1) and (2). Forward-looking goals, new products, new markets, and other objectives have never become so important as to distract the organization from the here-and-now goal of satisfying every customer on every element of every transaction.

The current management style includes assignment to each key staff member of responsibility for elements of profit and loss and the balance sheet plus clearcut responsibility (along departmental lines) for fulfillment of customer contracts. Since each customer order is a major portion of annual output, there is intimate involvement on the part of each key staff member with the customer as follows:

Sales coordinates and structures the sale with inputs from engineering, manufacturing, and finance as to specifications, shipping date, prices, and terms. Closing the order commits other key staff people to contractual obligations.

Engineering provides cost control, order processing management, and specifications, plus design work as needed.

Manufacturing provides cost and schedules contracts, quality control, and coordination of all suppliers.

Finance provides technical support through leasing options and cash planning.

Looking at the financial side, the company enjoys significant customer deposits on unshipped orders, which is an unusual feature of the business. In a sense this emphasizes the need for close attention to each customer, because the net effect of customer deposits is that the customer is lending money to Hantscho to help finance the manufacturing of the press order. This is an important source of working capital to the company on an "interest free" basis. Therefore it is imperative that managers and supervisors at all levels be totally aware of and committed to the goals and decision-making processes at work in the company.

Teamwork in the company is inspired by the tasks that must be completed to build quality products delivered on the precise dates specified in the contracts. Hantscho employees have a deep sense of loyalty to the company because they feel that their skills are used to build the products that are responsible for the continued growth and development of the business.

In this company the task track points to a progression from a statement at the top of the hierarchy of desired outcomes, to the assignment of missions and tasks, to public disclosure of intent, to frequent evaluation and reassessment of priorities. Because of their strong loyalties to the leader and their commitment to the organization's mission, managers placed task accomplishment (measured by *quality* of products produced and delivered to customers in a timely manner) at the head of their list of organizational concerns. Therefore teamwork was built and sustained around traditional workforce values. The role of management was clearly established along hierarchical principles of management. Decisions were made by authority and were highly centralized, definite, and unchallenged.

The organization's mission was established at the top of the hierarchy. Departmental and even individual goals were linked directly to the statement of mission established by the company's president. Employees at all levels in the structure were very clear about their roles and their specific work objectives. Commitment to the decisions made by management was very strong throughout the organization.

Product quality and business integrity (measured primarily by fair pricing, delivery on due date, and honesty in dealing with customers) stood as management's No. 1 concern. Individual and departmental performance was evaluated almost entirely on this basis. Interpersonal relations were subordinated to task accomplishment. Loyalty to the company was more important than loyalty to any one individual.

A task-oriented organization such as the Hantscho Company must rely on managers and employees who hold traditional values to achieve the organization's objectives. Teamwork can be built solely around organizational tasks when the workforce is composed of people who value loyalty, hierarchy, and other traditional values. Teamwork can be developed around tasks when a greater percentage of the workforce is concerned about progressing in a highly structured manner from a specific idea to a history of success. In the course of its history a task-oriented organization tends to build teamwork along a track similar to that in Figure 22.

Building Teamwork Around Relationships

Teamwork developed around relationships follows a very different track, as the following case illustrates.*

* All names and events have been altered to avoid revealing the actual identity of the company or any of its past or current employees.

BURGESS CASE

The Burgess Company was founded in the mid-1950s by R. A. Burgess, who set out to design and manufacture precision molded products for the medical and health service fields. Because of the immediate demand for these products, the company grew rapidly, adding manufacturing, marketing, purchasing, quality control, personnel, engineering, and research and development departments. By 1968 Burgess had become a leading supplier of molded products, with customers and offices located in several midwestern and mid-Atlantic states.

In 1972 Mr. Burgess decided to take early retirement. He turned the business over to Neal Harris, his vice-president of sales, who had established an excellent reputation for himself and his department with the company's customers. An outgoing, personable, and charismatic leader, Harris was viewed positively by most employees. Under his leadership the company continued to grow at an accelerated pace, opening up new sales offices in both the United States and Europe.

Harris was an excellent entrepreneur who devoted a good deal of time to the sales department and to customers. However, he paid scant attention to the details of managing the manufacturing and engineering functions, limiting himself to an occasional visit to the managers' offices, where he usually announced a new sale and congratulated the managers for getting the product out the door.

As the company increased its sales Harris expanded the sales force, promoted several managers in the department, and moved the main sales office to a new facility to accommodate this expansion and, in his words, to "create a better company image for the customer." With this increased status, the sales organization assumed a more aggressive role with the other departments. It established manufacturing timetables, insisted on the redesign of existing products, demanded new products and special orders delivered by specific times, and sold at prices that often did not account for purchase, development, and manufacturing costs. As a result, relationships between departments became tense and unproductive. Product quality diminished and manufacturing costs increased.

Recognizing that relationships were strained and that morale was declining rapidly, Harris initiated several actions designed to build teamwork.

1. He began a series of informal meetings and parties away from the office. He invited members of the sales department and a few select employees from the other functional areas and encouraged people to discuss their personal concerns. In return he expressed a concern for their individual welfare and made commitments to solve whatever problems they were experiencing.

2. He revised the merit compensation program and offered special bonuses to the sales department and to people who demonstrated that they were getting along with the sales force.

3. He brought selected individuals from each department together in order to surface interpersonal conflicts and to reassure these people that he wanted them on his team. He also encouraged them to play more golf together, to eat lunch together more often, and to travel together when on company business.

4. He stepped up his personal visits to employees at all levels of the organization and established a "completely open door policy," encouraging employees to seek him out and discuss any problem.

5. Through the informal communications network, he let it be known that the rewards for loyalty and cooperation would be job security, more responsibility, and more compensation.

6. He "loosened up" the organizational structure by (a) increasing the number of direct reporting relationships to himself and to the vice-president of sales, (b) communicating more directly with employees two and three levels down in the hierarchy, and (c) shifting certain work responsibilities "to individuals who would respond better to customer requirements."

As a result of these efforts, an in-group was created whose loyalties to Harris were unquestionable and whose power in the organization was uncontested. Led by the vice-president of sales, the in-group established the company's long-range plans, short-term objectives, and departmental budgets. The in-group then developed its own informal structure and norms and continued its domination of the decision-making process in the company. A strong sense of team spirit existed within the group. Conflicts were surfaced and dealt with openly. Plans and goals were designed using a consensus decision model. Responsibilities and assignments were discussed frequently. In short, Harris had succeeded in developing a team within the organization that appeared to be working together in a productive manner.

In 1974, two years after Harris was appointed, the company began to receive major complaints from its customers about the quality of one of its key product lines. As the number of complaints mounted, customers began to withhold payments, resulting in service cutbacks in product shipments. Within a short time, Burgess reappeared on the scene and began an investigation. It ultimately revealed that there were two teams in the organization—one headed by Harris and his in-group; the other by manufacturing and engineering personnel, who resented the in-group and who had retained a strong sense of loyalty to Burgess.

To help him solve the problem, Burgess retained a consulting firm that specialized in diagnosing and building teamwork through special application of conflict resolution techniques. After several months of group meetings and one-on-one sessions, the problems, instead of getting better, worsened.

Burgess then decided to move on his own. He immediately dismissed Harris, demoted the vice-president of sales, established parity in merit compensation, and redefined the company's missions. He then established new reporting relationships to himself and set specific objectives for each department to attain within specified periods of time. The momentum of the company shifted positively within eight months.

The strong sense of teamwork developed by Harris was based on psychological factors related to belonging, dependency, and counterdependency. In contrast to the Hantscho Company loyalty was established through personal rewards rather than through commitment to the organization's mission. Instead of focusing the attention of its managers on task accomplishment, the company's president created an environment in which the organization's membership was continually forced to deal with tensions related to interpersonal relations, such as those identified in the relationship track in Figure 23. Teamwork was built and sustained solely on the basis of interpersonal relationships. Management roles were determined by the "favorite son" phenomenon—the stronger the ties of friendship to the company's president, the larger the management responsibility.

Figure 22. Task track.

T_1	T_2	T_3	T_4	T_5	T_6
Leadership makes product/service decisions	Mission and expected outcomes identified	Norms and work rules established	Tasks assigned	Tasks performed	Task performance evaluated
INCEPTION	IDENTITY	STRUCTURES, ROLE NORMS	MANAGEMENT	ACTION	REVIEW

Figure 23. Relationship track.

R_1	R_2	R_3	R_4
In-out tensions; concerns about belonging and acceptance	Up-down tensions; dependency and counterdependency	Near-far tensions; conflict between members desiring intimacy and those desiring distance	Power tensions

R_5	R_6	R_7
Responsibility tensions; assignments and work loads—weighing of costs and rewards	Performance tensions; concerns for comparative evaluations	Image tensions; concerns for relationships

Decision making in the organization was also based on relationship. Decisions were made by minority rule. One, two, or three people in the sales department employed tactics that forced organizational decisions without the consent of the majority. Commitment to the decisions made by management was strong by the in-group, and almost nonexistent for members not included in this group.

The company's mission (for example, sales quotas for each salesman) was established at lower levels in the hierarchy and was communicated only to members of the in-group. With the exception of the field sales force, employees were not at all clear about their roles of their work objectives. Task accomplishment was always less important than interpersonal relations, and loyalty to the president and to the in-group counted more than loyalty to the company or to oneself.

Building teamwork solely on the basis of interpersonal relationships has dangerous organizational consequences. Where teamwork depends on the psychological and social needs of belonging and being accepted by a leader or by a group, interpersonal conflicts and destructive behavior are inevitable. Teamwork established along a relationship track generally succeeds neither with contemporary nor with traditional employees.

These two examples represent divergent management views on how to build effective teamwork. Neither approach produced optimum teamwork, but it is evident that the Hantscho task track style, based on traditional work values, produced better long-term operating results than the relationship style promoted by the president of the Burgess Company. Yet in today's environment it would be incorrect to assume that teamwork among traditional employees can be built along only one track. In the course of task achievement, team members typically address the questions of who's in charge, who's "in" or "out," and why interpersonal tensions exist. On the relationship level, teams may parallel the concerns on the task track while addressing (or failing to address) their concerns about acceptance, image, and power.

Building teamwork requires an understanding on the part of the manager and the team that their behavior should fluctuate from the task at hand to a concern for relationships. By achieving a proper balance between these two tracks, management can appeal to the values of both contemporary and traditional employees and thereby achieve the teamwork necessary to increase corporate profitability.

How to Build and Sustain Teamwork

Most efforts directed at building teamwork concentrate on issues related to the relationship track. It is frequently argued that issues along the relationship track often impede progress along the task track. Managers are therefore urged to invest the time and energy it takes to deal with conflicts, tensions, and other psychological needs. This argument has some merit, but it is also true that issues along the task track create relationship problems. Thus, instead of promoting the proliferation of techniques and approaches to build and sustain teamwork, management usually makes a wiser investment by directing the energies of its employees toward accomplishing specific tasks, dealing with relationship issues only when they seriously impede progress toward the company's goals.

The payoff for investing the time and effort to build teamwork comes when teams participate in solving business problems or creating innovations in technology, policy, or procedure. The guidelines that follow have proved successful in numerous situations in which managers have recognized the value of utilizing behavioral management principles to get the teamwork they need.

Step 1. Analyzing the team's work values

First, it is important to analyze the managers and their direct reports to determine the values they hold. This can be accomplished directly by administering the management or employee inventory discussed in Chapter 9 or indirectly by an interviewing process that discusses what the rules are that everyone in the organization should follow and what use the company makes of a person's experience and ideas. In the interview each manager might be asked to imagine that his or her work unit is a person, to describe that person, and to describe the ideal employee for the organization.

Building an information base that identifies the extent of the team's traditional and/or contemporary work values serves as the basis for determining a team-building strategy. Does the team value participative decision making? If so, it might be possible to build teamwork around group decision-making processes. Does the manager value personal loyalty while his or her subordinates value individuality? If so, teamwork may have to start with group sessions designed to resolve existing or potential conflicts over personal work values. Teamwork can successfully be established within a heterogeneous work group if team members have an understanding of each other's values. Although agreement is not always possible or even desirable, understanding is often a step toward empathy.

Step 2. Analyzing the team's task orientation

An analysis of the team's orientation toward task accomplishment should focus on its overall productivity as a work unit. In a manufacturing operation, for example, a study should be made of the production records in the plant, the work plan of the area, and safety, quality, and efficiency standards. In a sales department, factors such as increased volume, customer satisfaction, pricing decisions, and other profitability results should be assessed. This form of analysis can be conducted by a third party, by the team itself, or by a combination of a third party and the team.

Task analysis asks such questions as: What are the expected productivity outcomes for this team? How are decisions made? Are they carried out well? Are task assignments clear? How well has the team performed against the objectives? Do performance standards exist? Are they evaluated? Often it is advisable to extend this form of analysis beyond the immediate work unit to the employees themselves or to other work units. What do they see to be the problems in their own management hierarchy or in other work units with which they interface? How do they view productivity, efficiency, safety, and so on? Their self-assessment, together with the hard documentation on productivity, can be very beneficial in providing the team with further details on the problems and improvement opportunities available.

Step 3. Analyzing team relationships

The third step in the team-building process should include an analysis of the relationships among team members. As in step 2, this analysis can be done by a third party or by the team itself. Analyzing team relationships should address issues along the relationship track. Do team members feel a sense of belonging? Are there interpersonal conflicts that are impeding task accomplishment? Are there issues related to power? Is the work environment relatively free from tension? Do team members feel that the work is evenly distributed? Is there a sense of team spirit?

Obtaining a picture of the personal relationships within the team will help to formulate a team-development strategy. If, for example, team relationships are inhibiting goal attainment, the team should participate in activities that will reduce the conflict. Likewise, if there is an absence of trust in the team, this issue should be addressed by those affected. Relationship issues, however, should be dealt with only insofar as they adversely affect task attainment.

Step 4. Developing an operating philosophy

Analyzing team values, task accomplishment, and relationships should lead the team into an examination of its existing philosophy and ultimately to a statement of its preferred philosophy. Getting team members to agree on operating principles forces them to reveal publicly the assumptions about human behavior on which they base their actions. This is the critical stage in building teams.

The team approach to management requires more than an occasional nod to the principles of good teamwork. To be successful, the team approach requires a commitment to a management philosophy that makes people work together within the framework of profitability goals. Therefore the team should design and communicate an operating philosophy that outlines the behavioral principles it intends to allow in the conduct of its business. Below is an example of an operating philosophy that was drawn up by a plant manager and his team.

TEAM OPERATING PHILOSOPHY

The management philosophy of the plant is one that has evolved through seven years of operation. It is based on four important value assumptions.

1. People will put forth the energy necessary to reach goals they helped to identify.
2. Cooperative interdependence of all personnel is an inherent characteristic of the production process within the plant.
3. People can and do act either to help or to hinder production, depending on their perception of the degree of compatibility between personnel and plant work requirements (goals, processes, and procedures).
4. Voluntary commitment to the plant's work processes is essential both to job satisfaction for the employee and to efficient productivity in the plant.

Because of the belief in these assumptions, the management philosophy is seen as essentially based on team activity. Just as the production processes related to a given product are interdependent, so are the work activities of the employees. By nature, the work requires a team approach to an identification of problems and voluntary synergistic effort toward resolution.

Everybody, given their level of responsibility, technical competence, and tasks, must have input to the problem-solving processes, since each team member is in the best position to assess production process needs in his or her area of responsibility. If people are not consulted or refuse to contribute, production will suffer.

Decision making cannot be viewed as the sole prerogative of management. Each person must make decisions moment by moment at any point in the production process. Only the type of decision varies from level to level. Therefore, managers, professionals, administrators, and technicians must have input on problems commensurate with their degree and type of involvement in the production and support processes of the plant. Adequate energy for this type of involvement is seen as a result of psychological ownership of any given plant objective(s).

The function of the plant's management is to make these kinds of team activities happen within the framework outlined in the four assumptions.

The values held by this team are reflected in their desire to include every team member in the problem-solving and decision-making process. A statement of operating philosophy will not prevent problems related to task accomplishment or team relationships, but it can be a valuable asset in clarifying key operating procedures related to planning, problem solving, and decision making.

Step 5. Measuring team results

For a team to function effectively it must know how well it is doing. Step 5 in developing teamwork should involve the team in a process to establish criteria that can be used to measure performance on a regular basis. The criteria should be built around task and relationship measures. This can be done by soliciting inputs from both the people who make up the work unit and the people outside the work unit who exercise management control over the work.

In the case of one very successful team effort aimed at improving productivity in a manufacturing plant with approximately 250 employees, the plant manager and his staff agreed on five major criteria for evaluating the team's progress over a one-year period. These criteria were:

1. Improvement in productivity as measured in pounds per unit per month.
2. Decrease in the amount of waste material as measured by the amount discarded and carried away from the plant each month.
3. Improvements in the staff meetings as measured by management and consultant perception of (a) time spent in the meetings, (b) quality of decisions arrived at, (c) amount of time devoted to implementing the decisions, and (d) effect of the decisions on plant operations.
4. Improvement in plant morale as measured by employees' perceptions of management's treatment of employees, communications, and developmental opportunities.
5. A significant improvement in the plant management's team behavior as measured by ten agreed-upon behavioral norms.

The development of performance measures serves the important purpose of providing feedback to the team on its individual and collective efforts. In some organizations, merit compensation is linked more to team performance than to individual performance.

Step 6. Using team meetings to solve problems

Is a team more effective at solving problems than individuals? A number of experiments on group and individual effectiveness over the past 35 years have failed to resolve this question. It is generally agreed, however, that a team that functions well has the potential of doing better than a single superior individual. For the best work to be done and for relationships to be built around organizational rather than personal issues, it is necessary to involve teams in identifying and resolving business problems.

Before solving problems it is necessary first to introduce a simple problem-solving and decision-making process that can be used by the team to surface and analyze business problems or opportunities. Research concerning productive task-oriented groups suggests that an organized (yet flexible) process for problem solving increases the likelihood that a team will reach its goals without overlooking vital considerations. Although a team should follow some type of structured process in its thinking, a variety of patterns for that process have been developed and have produced quality solutions. No single pattern emerged as the best under all circumstances.

It is also important to establish behavioral norms or rules of conduct for team meetings. The norms listed below are offered as examples for teams to follow in managing their behavior as they work on specific tasks.

Strive toward consensus in making decisions.

Focus conflict on ideas rather than individuals.

Establish clear goals for each team meeting.

Evaluate progress often, using both qualitative and quantitative measures.

Openly voice feeling on issues (not people).

Express commitment or noncommitment openly.

Allow for changes in leadership roles during team discussion.

Avoid separate discussions and interruptions during team meetings.

Some teams find it helpful to develop their own norms and continually evaluate their behavior, using some method of quantifying their perceptions of their effectiveness. Then by using their own norms as guides to group behavior, they can preserve healthy relationships better while working toward correcting those that are deficient.

Step 7. Developing the team's analytical capability

Most successful team efforts are initiated and sustained by frequent assessments of both task and relationship issues. This can be done by developing a uniform approach to collecting information from the workforce on a systematic and continuing basis. There are several advantages to developing and implementing a uniform approach.

First, a uniform data collection approach enables the team to surface latent issues that should be dealt with in group settings. This is true whether the issues and problems are with a person, a team, or an entire organization. When you uncover these issues, they become public; that is, they are brought outside the individual and the team. They then become legitimate materials with which to deal, to discuss, to try to correct, or to improve.

A second advantage to collecting data in a uniform manner is that it allows the team to focus its energies and time on the appropriate material and to control the list, to a limited extent, of things that are dealt with in team meetings. In this way, the team is able to ensure that crucial existing issues are worked on rather than less important ones that members may use to avoid grappling with the more uncomfortable ones.

Third, collecting information systematically and frequently makes it possible to provide feedback to an individual, team, or organization in a way that is characterized by relatively low threat. When people get information from a questionnaire they have filled out or an interview in which they have participated, they are more likely to trust the information than if they receive it in a random manner.

Last, uniform data collection allows for longitudinal assessment of change in a person, team, or organization. This assessment can be useful in demonstrating that building effective teamwork contributes significantly to the goals management has set for the organization.

Beyond these specific steps for building teamwork, management must make a sincere commitment to the values inherent in the concept itself—participative planning and decision making, self-analysis and feedback, openness and trust in communications, and so forth. This cannot be done without a continuous effort. Furthermore, team building should not begin or end at any one level in the organization. It is important that teamwork include vertical, horizontal, and in some instances diagonal groupings. The stated management philosophy must be brought down through the organization if the team approach is to be successful. Also, building a team must be accepted as a management responsibility rather than just another technique or fad to try for a few days every year or so.

Summary

The team approach, is used wisely, enables management to obtain high performance standards by raising the consciousness and commitment of individuals and groups to increased productivity. Good teamwork developed and sustained along a track that balances task concerns with relationship issues will unite people in a basic cause to which they will be highly committed.

Effective teamwork is a necessary component of organizational life. An understanding by management at all levels in the hierarchy of the dynamics present in the task and relationship tracks can improve both the productivity and psychological well-being of team members. Building teamwork, therefore, requires a commitment first, to improving the quantity and quality of work, and second, to increasing team member relationships.

You cannot build teamwork throughout an organization without management's support of the values inherent in the team concept. Using teams to plan, to make decisions, to identify and solve problems, and to assist with the management process itself often requires a major change in organizational policies and practices. How can this change be achieved? Chapter 14 outlines an approach for introducing change within an organization that, if successful, can make teamwork a reality.

14

Improving
employee productivity

TODAY'S TREND in management toward more sophisticated management controls is paralleled by a significant decrease in the level of motivation in the workforce. Currently, only 13 percent of the labor force finds its work meaningful. Whereas in the 1950s workers gained their respectability from working (masculinity was defined as being a good provider), now 64 percent of the labor force tries to define its sense of self away from the work environment. Today's workforce must be characterized as "seekers of pleasures." People want to be excited, invigorated; they want to move away from the routine.

While behavioral scientists are arguing that employee values have changed, that workers want more participation and freedom in the job, management has created elaborate control systems to enable them to obtain finite measures of productivity, account for costs, and exercise tight control over work output. These systems may be invaluable for management information and decision-making purposes, but they have created an adversary relationship between management and workers. The move toward more sophisticated control systems is supported by managers who attempt to compel higher productivity from the workforce to help achieve management's goals.

In most organizations productivity improvements are the sole responsibility of management. Typically the labor force has little or no voice in the decision processes used to gain greater work output. The use of such practices as work measurement, systems performance evaluation, and exception reports are intended to identify differences in productivity and substandard employee performance. These approaches appear logical and in some instances are quite effective, but the cost of maintaining the control system necessary to ensure their effectiveness is high. Clerks, technical personnel, supervisors, and the computer are all a necessary part of implementing and auditing these systems, at considerable expense to the organization. Still, major efforts continue to establish more controls in a work environment in which employees are not motivated to increase their work output.

Attempts to increase worker productivity by a variety of approaches aimed at gaining a commitment to management's productivity objectives have been largely ineffective. In 1978, the productivity of the American economy increased by less than 1 percent. In the past ten years, the national productivity rate has fallen to slightly less than half its historic trend of 3.2 percent. The 1979 Economic Report to the President offers little hope for the immediate future, even to the optimist. The report projects an average increase in productivity of slightly less than 1.5 percent for the economy to 1983.

The reasons for the decrease in productivity growth in our country are complex and probably not fully understood even by the most enlightened sources. The decline has been attributed to the following factors:

Shifts in the industrial composition of the economy.
Changes in the composition of the labor force.
The trend to supplement capital equipment investment with increases in the labor force.
Leveling off of research and development expenditures.
Diversion of investment to pollution abatement expenditures.

Changes in worker attitudes toward work.

Development of little new technology in mature industries.

Shift to a service-oriented economy.

High investments in energy-saving or -conversion facilities because of higher energy costs.

Economists and labor analysts have provided an interesting inventory of reasons for the steady decline in productivity growth. Still, the human factor in productivity remains as perhaps the largest, most misunderstood, contributor. Productivity studies show that the human factor contributes from 10 to 25 percent to productivity growth. It often exceeds 50 percent of controllable costs. In labor-intensive service and government, people account for 20 to 85 percent of all costs. The decline in the rate of productivity growth cannot be rationalized purely in terms of capital and research factors. The human factor in the productivity equation provides management with one of the more hopeful responses to our productivity problem.

In this chapter we shall examine the effectiveness of the more frequently used approaches to motivate workers toward increased productivity and shall propose an alternative approach that has proved successful in a number of organizations.

Conventional Motivational Approaches

In the past several years it has become fashionable to blame productivity problems on management's lack of finesse in obtaining results from the workforce. The popularity of management by objectives (MBO) is the result of management's awareness of the necessity of establishing objectives to serve as a standard for measuring individual and group performance. In more recent years the idea of a performance appraisal program has taken root; managers are required to evaluate the performance of employees regularly on the basis of preestablished work expectations.

These approaches can be an effective means of organizing and evaluating the work of management, but they are largely ineffectual as a means of increasing the overall productivity of a group. MBO and other related approaches are based on the assumption that productivity increases can be achieved if each employee fully understands what is expected from him.

MBO and performance appraisal programs are supported by compensation systems that reward only individual merit. The conventional wage incentive programs reinforce the idea that each employee should focus only on his or her objectives. Employees on such incentives often do attempt to increase their own work output, but they are not motivated to raise the organization's overall level of productivity or to cooperate with employees outside their own work group. In most companies incentives are offered only to part of the workforce, on the premise that so-called "nonproductive" work cannot be measured. Conventional incentive programs usually divide the workforce into two camps—those on incentives and those who are not included.

Merit-rating programs are often effective for the employee without long-term service. Because most merit programs have a ceiling, practically all long-service employees are at or near the top and thus have little incentive to increase productivity. Merit programs also tend to fractionalize the workforce in that only a small percentage of workers are rewarded at any time.

The suggestion plan, which rewards employees who contribute valid ideas, is widely used in some organizations as an incentive for productivity improvement. Most suggestion plans are short lived, however, and do not promote employee involvement and cooperation over time. Mitchell Fein tells of a case worth citing.

A well-known large company pays good wages and has excellent relations with its employees and the union. Its suggestion plan paid employees 15 percent of a year's savings, with a policy of no layoffs due to improvements from suggestions. An employee developed improvements which eliminated three assemblers from each of six lines and received a cash reward of $24,000. All

18 displaced employees were given their choice of other jobs and their union seniority was fully protected. Management was proud of its innovative employee and he received wide publicity. Some employees were not impressed; the award winner also received a truckload of wet concrete on his driveway and the windows of his house were smashed. Though no one lost his job, some employees apparently felt that 18 jobs had been lost to the plant.*

Although suggestion programs have some utility, they often build resentment, because they single out individuals and reward them while the rest of the workforce looks on. Suggestion plans usually lose their value as a result of peer pressure and the ire of workers against suggestion innovators.

Requisites for Improved Productivity

The motivational programs patterned after Abraham Maslow's hierarchy of needs have received a great deal of attention in management literature. Programs to enrich jobs, enlarge jobs, rotate jobs, and restructure jobs have been promoted in the literature as significant breakthroughs in increasing worker motivation and improving productivity. The early reports from such companies as Texas Instruments, General Foods, Corning Glass, and others who experimented with these approaches seemed to hold promise of a behavioral science breakthrough in productivity experiments. However, with only minor exceptions, these approaches have had little or no impact in increasing employee motivation and productivity.

Despite the apparent failure of these behavioral science experiments, they have produced some valuable insights related to worker productivity. Of all the factors that contribute to the creation of a highly motivated and productive workforce, the principal one is that management must recognize and reward effective per-

* From an unpublished paper, 1977.

formance. A National Science Foundation study team concluded after an extensive study of worker motivation and productivity that "financial compensation of workers must be linked to their performance and to productivity gains." When workers' pay is linked to their performance, their motivation to work increases, their productivity is higher, and they are more satisfied with their work.

In a study conducted by Mitchell Fein of over 400 manufacturing plants in the United States, he found that when management instituted work measurement, the plant's productivity rose an average of 14.6 percent. When management instituted wage incentives where work measurements already existed, productivity rose an average of 42.9 percent. The average increase from no measurement to incentives was almost 64 percent.

Most behavioral management approaches have rejected the notion that money motivates, but the fact remains that management has long recognized the value of tying pay to productivity performance. A study of over 1,100 companies listed on the New York Stock Exchange found that companies with formal incentive plans for their executives earned an average of almost 44 percent more pretax profit than nonincentive companies did. Managers responsible for sales also recognize the importance of tying pay to performance. According to a Conference Board study, from two-thirds to three-quarters of all the sales forces in the United States use incentives.

Linking financial rewards to productivity may be the most powerful motivator to improving the overall performance of the workforce. Yet only 26 percent of workers in the United States work under financial incentives. In some industries (for example, steel), over 80 percent of the workforce is on incentives, but in many industries no incentives are employed.

What accounts for management's apparent reluctance to use financial incentives? Some managers are concerned that financial incentives will erode their ability to control operations and that over a period of time incentives will deteriorate. Others believe that improvements in productivity are largely the result of management efforts and therefore are not willing to share the rewards for productivity gains. Still others believe that periodic increases in wages and benefits are sufficient motivators. There may be some merit to these arguments, but a substantial body of knowledge supports the thesis that if workers are to cooperate in productivity improvement, they must benefit financially from the gains associated with these improvements.

A second important factor for increasing worker productivity is job security. Typically a professional or managerial employee does not work himself out of a job by increasing his overall effectiveness and efficiency. A salesman does not fear for his job if he sells too much. A controller is not laid off if he introduces systems and procedures that reduce or eliminate the amount of time he spends preparing financial reports. On the contrary, these employees are usually rewarded for their creativity and effectiveness.

In many instances, however, hourly employees are penalized for their creative efforts. If they improve productivity, reduce downtime, or improve their own efficiency, they are often displaced because they have "proved" to management that the operation can run with fewer employees. Unlike executives or salesmen, they receive no reinforcement that their efforts will benefit them in the future. It is paradoxical to expect employees to be committed to increasing productivity if their own job security or the security of their co-workers is threatened.

Often, without even realizing it, management offers its employees the opportunity of reduced job security for their efforts to improve productivity. To ensure worker commitment to productivity improvement, management must guarantee employees job security. An effective productivity sharing plan can assist management with this task. A look at the oldest productivity sharing plan, the Scanlon Plan, provides valuable insight into the process of establishing a tailor-made program.

The Scanlon Plan

In the late 1930s Joseph Scanlon led the fight to organize the United Steel Workers of America. Faced with the real possibility of bankruptcy, the owner of U.S. Steel accompanied Scanlon on a visit to the union's headquarters in Pittsburgh in a kind of last-ditch effort to save the company. In conversations with the regional director responsible for Scanlon's local union, the owner learned that the workers in the plant were more than willing to increase production if a way could be found to enlist their support. Later Scanlon returned to the plant and interviewed workers on how to improve production. Ultimately, the plant was saved and a productivity sharing plan, the Scanlon Plan, was born.

The Scanlon Plan was the first sharing plan that tied a financial incentive to organized productivity. Through a committee system of workers and managers and a philosophy of participative management, workers and managers generate ideas and turn these ideas into actions that lead to productivity increases. A monthly bonus is paid to all workers and managers for increases in labor productivity. A historical ratio of labor costs to the sales value of production is generally tied to each month's output. Most of the savings below expected labor costs are distributed to workers in proportion to their regular earnings. Some portion of the savings—typically 25 percent—is returned to the company as an incentive for its adopting the plan.

In spite of the early success of the Scanlon Plan few companies have adopted its use. James Driscoll, in discussing the current status of the plan, indicates that "Probably 50 to 100 unionized plants in the U.S. and Canada owned by a smaller number of separate companies currently use the plan. Fewer nonunion plants use the Scanlon Plan, tending to use other forms of profit or gain sharing."

The low use of the Scanlon Plan is generally attributable to its inflexibility in establishing productivity measurements. The Scanlon Plan sets a single ratio of dollar labor payroll to dollar sales shipments for the entire business. With changes in product mix, market conditions, and labor contract settlements, the productivity measurements become distorted. It is often difficult to factor out changes in technology and capital equipment. Because employees will accept only changes that work for them, a new ratio must be negotiated every time an organizational or economic factor affects the base measurement.

The Scanlon Plan has obvious limitations, but it does serve as the basis for many of the plans that have followed. One plan that has proved effective borrows the Scanlon concept of productivity sharing but departs significantly from his method of implementation.

A New Plan

In recent years a new type of sharing plan has been developed by Mitchell Fein. It is directed at the needs and objectives of management and workers. To differentiate this plan from others, Fein named it the Improshare Plan. The name is derived from the phrase "improved productivity through sharing." The plan is designed to remove the traditional limitations on productivity improvements.

The Improshare Plan establishes a common objective for both management and workers: more units of product produced in fewer man-hours of work. The motivation to achieve this objective is based on a reward system that both interest groups share in common. Financial incentives are linked directly to both individual performance and productivity gains. Narrow interests under this plan are reduced in that the entire work group is rewarded for gains. The plan has these additional elements:

1. Every member of a defined work group (such as a plant, department, or division) shares in the gains.
2. Past average productivity levels are used as a base against

which improvement can be measured. The average number of man-hours required to produce a unit of product in a specified time period is established as the standard for measuring productivity. The standard is determined by calculating the average output level over a period of several weeks. Losses are then absorbed into this average.

3. Productivity is measured as the hour value of output measured against the total hours worked by the group. In an organization with multiple products, the total work output is the sum of all the products completed multiplied by their respective standards.

4. Production is counted only for acceptable pieces in a finished state ready to ship or assemble.

5. Productivity improvement is shared equally between employees and the company.

6. Productivity gains are calculated and paid weekly.

7. Increased productivity is shared with no attempt to pinpoint whether employees or managers created the savings.

8. A ceiling on productivity is established to cap how much the company pays out. Management buys back (through cash payments) the standard(s) if productivity is sustained or increased beyond the capped level.

9. Standards are not changed when operations are changed by either management or employees except for capital equipment and technology changes, which are specifically defined.

10. The total unit man-hour costs under the plan cannot exceed past unit costs. As productivity increases, costs must decrease.

11. Management maintains its rights to manage. All changes in methods, quality, production levels, schedules, employee assignments, hiring, firing, and so on are fully vested in management.

12. Union contract agreements are not altered.

The Improshare Plan makes it possible for workers to share management's objectives. As their attention is focused on the final outcome of their efforts, they become more interested in the day-to-day problems and opportunities. Since productivity gains are shared, workers and management alike begin to pay attention to the impediments in production that occur around them, impediments they might have ignored or even encouraged before. The goal of the plan is to involve all employees. Individual performance is not singled out and rewarded, but the outstanding benefit of the plan is that every employee benefits from a team effort aimed at increasing total productivity.

Experiences with Improshare Plans

The first Improshare Plan was established in August 1974 in a furniture-manufacturing company. Productivity increased so rapidly that the measurement standard had to be raised twice. This meant that management had to reimburse workers for achieving productivity levels that exceeded the standard by 60 percent. Today, employees are earning 30 percent more pay. In addition, production costs have been reduced substantially.

A national corrugated container company installed Improshare Plans in four of its plants. Management then weighed the results obtained through Improshare with the results in its other plants, which operated with conventional incentives. After a year's operation the plants on Improshare outperformed even the most effective incentive plants. The average increase in productivity was 31 percent. Management controls were greatly simplified. The labor climate and employee attitudes showed improvement.

An industrial products company introduced Improshare Plans by product line and by major operation. The manufacturing operation of one product line increased output by 18 percent and reduced scrap from 17 percent to 7 percent in a matter of months. Still another operation increased output by 54 percent while increasing quality also.

Before installing Improshare, a small consumer products company was forced to defer wage increases for a year because of its poor financial condition. Management had demonstrated this problem to the union during contract negotiations and the wage deferment plan was agreed upon. The Improshare Plan was then installed. Employees are earning more than they would have through a wage increase.

A large company used the Improshare Plan to improve the productivity of its construction crew, which was responsible for erecting new buildings. The plan covered 150 construction mechanics and their supervisors and managers. In the first six months, productivity increased by 16 percent as a result of improvements in the planning process.

An automobile parts plant with a workforce of 500 was ready to discontinue a product line because of excessive costs and continual quality problems. The Improshare Plan was introduced as a replacement for a conventional incentive plan that covered 75 employees. After one week, productivity increased and quality improved. In one instance, the machine operators shut down their machines, called engineering and quality control, and informed it that the machines would not operate until efficiency and quality improvements were made. As a result, costs were reduced and the product line was saved.

In spite of the success of the Improshare Plan, some companies have failed in their attempts to use it. One company tried to replace an ineffective incentive plan with Improshare in a department with six separate groups that assembled and packed products. Under the incentive plan, each group had its own standard and was paid for its own productivity. When Improshare was introduced, the entire work output of the department was grouped under a single standard of measurement.

The plan failed because employees were accustomed to work as small groups. Most refused to pool their output and share their work with others. The company learned in retrospect that combining six groups into one larger group was artificial and uncomfortable from the employees' point of view. A reluctance to share output among members of a large work group is often a serious obstacle to the success of the Improshare Plan.

Companies that have not communicated the purpose of the plan to employees have had the least success. If the plan is viewed as a new form of piecework or a management gimmick to get employees to work harder, it is destined for failure. The most important factor affecting the success of the plan is open communication between management and employees. Management's willingness to be candid with information on productivity levels, incoming orders, future changes, organizational problems, and so forth is essential. The type of climate created by management before, during, and after the installation of the program will greatly affect its success.

How to Install a Productivity Sharing Plan

Step 1. Establish a measurement base

The first step in installing a productivity sharing plan is to establish the measurement base. It should be remembered that a productivity sharing plan can be developed for any operation. The number of people in the work unit is irrelevant. A properly designed plan can be applied to one person, to a small group, to a department, or to an entire plant. The versatility of the Improshare Plan, for example, comes from the way productivity is measured, namely, hours of output versus hours of input.

The Improshare Plan makes use of a variety of measurement methods. The categories of measurement include:

Gross measures for an entire facility, for a plant, for nonincentive operations in a conventional incentive plant, or for supplementing conventional incentive programs.

Estimated standards for job shop products or proprietary products.

Conventional work measurement standards that are applied
plantwide or by department and groups.
Measurement of actual costs by products in a single plant or in
a group of plants.

The Improshare Plan can be used in combination with conventional incentives to include employees who are not covered,
such as those in shipping, maintenance, warehouse, and materials
handling. The incentives for the production operations do not
need to be changed. Improshare plans can be established for non-
production operations using the past year's average of man-hours
per finished unit of product. This approach may be inexact when
compared with engineered standards, but a study of historical data
indicates that the past year's average is usually a reliable base.

Determining how to measure has traditionally been one of the
most difficult problems associated with conventional incentive
programs. Since measurement is difficult, most incentive plans
cover only a portion of workers in an organization, eliminating the
so-called "nonproductive" work, such as maintenance, materials
handling, and other departments not directly involved in production. To establish a measurement base that includes all employees
in a work group, the total output of the group against the total
hours worked by the group can serve as a valid measurement base.
This principle can be demonstrated in the following example:

A single-product plant of 100 employees produced 26,000 units
over a 26-week period in which they worked a total of 104,000
hours. The average time per unit is $104,000/26,000 = 4.0$ hours.
Suppose an Improshare Plan is introduced under which the employees and management share productivity gains equally below
the past cost of 4.0 hours per unit. In a given week, if 102 employees worked a total of 4,080 hours and produced 1,300 units, the
value of the output would be $1,300 \times 4.0$ hours per unit $= 5,200$
hours. The gain would be $5,200 - 4,080 = 1,120$ hours, with one-
half or 560 hours going to the employees. Translated into pay, this
would be $560/4,080 = 13.7$ percent additional pay to each em-

ployee. Management also would gain 560 hours. Where originally the unit cost was 4.0 hours, the new unit cost, including productivity sharing payments, is: $(4,080 + 560)/1,300 = 3.57$ hours. Thus costs have been reduced, in spite of productivity sharing payments to the employees.

In plants with more than one product, a measurement base must be established that will reflect the past average productivity for all products and for the entire plant. The specific methodology for establishing standards in plants with multiple products must be tailored to the size of the operation and the number of products.

Step 2. Establish ceiling and buy-back principles

Improshare standards are protected by a ceiling on productivity sharing earnings and a buy back of productivity over the ceiling. The ceiling and buy-back principles are the mainstays of the Improshare Plan.

The controls work as follows: Suppose a 50-50 sharing plan has a 30 percent ceiling on incentive earnings, which is 160 percent productivity. When productivity averages 180 percent, the excess of 20 percentage points is "banked" for future weeks. If productivity remains over the ceiling, the standards can be bought back with the employees' agreement. All the time standards involved are reduced by a factor so that, in this case, 180 percent becomes 160 percent.

The employees receive a cash payment of 50 percent of the 20 percent, projected for a year, at their regular pay (because this is a 50 percent sharing plan). A \$5.00-an-hour employee would receive a cash payment of $\$5.00 \times 2,000$ hours $\times 50$ percent $\times 20$ percent = \$1,000. This buy back is for management's right to change the product standards. Simultaneous with the buy back all time standards are reduced by a multiplier of $1.6/1.8 = 0.8889$. The ceiling and buy back can also be used for conventionally established time standards.

The controls necessary for conventional time standards actually inhibit increased productivity, because workers resist changes in standards; they hide their methods improvements. When management makes standards changes, workers receive no benefits. With the Improshare Plan workers receive 50 percent of productivity gains and when standards are bought back they receive large cash bonuses. They have every reason to aid management in introducing changes and to contribute their own ideas. The ceiling and buy back will control Improshare standards far more effectively than traditional methods can.

Conventional time standards are designed to operate in an adversary relations system. Standards for measured day work are management's definitions of a fair day's work and are used to enforce a productivity level it believes is reasonable. Standards for conventional incentives are based on the fair day's work concept but offer increased earnings opportunities to employees who exceed the standards. Those who do not achieve the standards may face disciplinary actions.

Improshare standards are not based on the traditional fair day's work concept. Its standards are used only to measure productivity improvement and to share productivity gains, not to coerce workers to higher levels. This difference between conventional time standards and Improshare standards is the key to understanding the role of standards in a work environment. The detailed microelements of conventional standards and the need to control standards against deterioration are necessary for these measurements to operate. Broad, gross standards are valid and necessary for Improshare. Those concerned with work measurement must comprehend the measurement needs of the two different work environment systems.

Step 3. Communicate the program to employees

In most conventional incentive plans time standards are set by management for each element of the operation. Management defines these standards by the work required to make the pieces rather than by the units produced per hour. Once the standards have been set, emphasis is placed on controlling them in order to ensure against erosion of the measurement system.

Conventional work measurement is microoriented; standards are measured in thousandths of a minute. When a change is made either by an employee or management in how an operation is performed, the standard is revised to reflect the change in order to protect the system itself. Under this approach, employees gain by hiding their improvements. Instead of producing more, employees conceal changes from management and create more idle time for themselves.

It is essential, therefore, to be sure that employees understand the key principles of the Improshare Plan before proceeding with its installation. Employees should be informed through group meetings, one-on-one discussions, and formal written communications that Improshare measures are macrostandards for finished product ready for shipping, totaling all operations. It is equally essential that management explain the ceiling and buy-back principles.

Step 4. Evaluate employees' perception of their own productivity

Following a carefully designed communications program on the purpose of the Improshare Plan, management should systematically gather some information regarding employees' perception of their own productivity. To facilitate this process, a written questionnaire should be administered to all employees in the work unit. The questionnaire should contain information such as the following:

How much effort do you expend on a day-to-day basis?
Less than 50 percent
About 50 percent
60 to 70 percent
75 percent

80 to 90 percent
100 percent

How much of your effort is lost or unproductive?
55 percent or more
50 percent
30 to 45 percent
About 25 percent
Less than 25 percent
Very little (about 5 percent)
None of my effort

Estimate your capacity for increased productivity.
More than 50 percent
About 50 percent
About 25 percent
About 15 percent
About 5 percent
None at all

My work load needs to be:
Increased by about 25–40 percent
Increased by about 10 percent
Neither increased nor decreased
Decreased by about 10 percent
Decreased by about 25–40 percent

After productivity data have been gathered, they should be fed back to employees in small group meetings. These sessions should focus on the overall results of the survey and should bring employees into a discussion on the merits of a productivity sharing program.

Asking employees to evaluate their own productivity anonymously provides management with a base line of information that can be used for setting productivity goals. Involving employees in the process of self-analysis serves the further purpose of heightening employee attention to productivity issues.

Step 5. Provide employees with job security

A program for productivity improvement must provide for workers' job security. Though management cannot completely protect against economic downturns such as the one in 1980, there is much that can be done. Since job security is such an important component of the work environment, managers must look upon it as an essential precondition to enhancing the will to work. The idea that economic insecurity is a restraint on the will to work is not new, but its effect is often minimized by managers, behavioral scientists, and industrial engineers working on productivity improvement. Job security is as vital to productivity improvement as advanced technical processes and new equipment.

Managers must view job security not only in the social sense of how it affects workers' lives, but also as absolutely essential to high levels of productivity. In plants without job security, workers stretch out the work if they do not see enough forthcoming. They will not work themselves out of their jobs. When workers stretch out their jobs, it is reflected in costs.

Managers historically have considered job security as a union demand to be bargained for during union negotiations. This has been a tragic error. Whenever job security is lacking, labor productivity is restrained. Paradoxically, managers should demand employee job security if they hope to increase productivity. What would happen in contract negotiations if management started off by demanding that the new contract include job protection for the employees? This radical act might encourage profound changes in employees' attitudes.

Productivity sharing provides employees with the opportunity to help assure their job security by assisting in raising productivity and reducing costs. In a competitive market even small cost reductions can make a big difference in being able to secure new orders. In the final analysis, the best assurance of income protection is in working for a profitable company that stays in business.

Summary

Productivity sharing is an alternative to traditional authoritarian managing. The Improshare Plan develops conditions and practices that are diametrically opposed to the tight cost control methods conventionally employed to raise productivity.

Traditional managing requires exact time standards, individual employee measurements, job descriptions, and detailed job instructions to assure that workers perform effectively. Increased productivity does not directly benefit workers. Improshare establishes a loosely structured environment in which workers perform effectively because they benefit directly from their efforts.

Traditional managing does not rely on worker cooperation; managers marshal their resources and act unilaterally to achieve management's goals. The Improshare Plan rewards employees for helping to achieve a primary management goal: more units of production or service output with less units of labor input. Congruent goals can be developed through Improshare Plans that will enable workers and management to work together for mutual gain.

Satisfaction of people with the work they do cannot be turned on or off by manipulating job content or proclaiming a new era of worker participation in decision making. Workers' attitudes are formed from their experiences and by what they want from their work. Each person has the right to shape his own values and seek fulfillment in his own terms. A democratic society should strive for greater freedom in all aspects of its citizens' lives and for assurances against deprivation and job insecurity.

Managers must become more aware of workers' total needs and create opportunities that workers will view as beneficial to them. As workers and managers perceive that there is more to be gained from cooperation than from conflict, they will find accommodating ways.

The road to increased productivity is so simple it often alludes us. Increase workers' will to work by rewarding them for more effective performance. Simultaneously, eliminate practices that penalize them as they progress. This is all that need be done. The productivity sharing described in this chapter is the essence of simplicity: Share productivity gains, starting with today's labor costs. The only magic in the plan is what workers and management put into it—the will to gain together.

NOTES

The research reported in this chapter has been published in the following sources:

R. A. Katzell, D. Yankelovich, M. Fein, O. A., Ornati, and A. Nash, *Work, Productivity, and Job Satisfaction.* New York: The Psychological Corporation, 1975.

Mitchell Fein, "Work Measurement and Wage Incentives," *Industrial Engineering,* September 1973

L. J. Brindisi, "Survey of Executive Compensation," *World,* Spring 1971.

D. A. Weeks, "Compensating Salesmen and the Salesforce," The Conference Board, Report No. 706, 1976.

James W. Driscoll, "Working Creatively with a Union: Lesson from the Scanlon Plan," *Organizational Dynamics,* Summer 1979.

Improshare is the registered service name used by Mitchell Fein. The experiences with Improshare have been recorded by Mitchell Fein, who has installed Improshare Plans in some of the largest organizations in this country and the rest of the world.

15

A human resource approach to managing

THE PRECEDING CHAPTERS in Part III have outlined the need for major changes that management must consider to attract, develop, and motivate people in a productive manner. The economic, technological, and sociopolitical changes that will occur in the 1980s will profoundly affect the management of our human resources. To implement the approaches outlined in this section, management must begin with a plan for their operation that integrates philosophy with practice. Administering an attitude survey to a group of employees, for example, should not be done without their clear understanding that obtaining their views on selected organizational issues is an integral part of a management philosophy that supports upward communications and endorses employee participation in problem solving. A human resource plan is an essential first step to implementing programs designed to achieve a high return on management's investment in people.

This chapter consists of an example of a human resource plan that was developed for a start-up plant in the Donaldson Company. The document, entitled "A Human Resource Approach to Managing: A Plant Manager's Guide," was developed in concert with the division's top management as well as the management in the plant. It is intended as a planning tool and information source to guide the plant's policies, programs, and management practices. The appropriate sections of the guide have been reviewed with each employee.

Management Philosophy

Employees are the largest nonfinancial resource which the Donaldson Company can utilize in achieving its business objectives. The way in which the company manages this resource can materially affect the company's profitability and its attractiveness as a place to work. Therefore, sound human resource management and progressive employee relations practices are necessary at all levels in the organization to ensure a superior return on the human resource investment, as well as the maintenance of a highly desirable quality of work life for employees.

It is not the purpose of this document to explore complex philosophies of managing, nor to compress years of management science into a few pages. Rather, those elements of management style which represent progressive human resource management are advanced as a guide to managing the plant.

These elements of management style include a number of assumptions, policies, programs, and procedures which are designed to assist in the attainment of business objectives, as well as to meet the needs of employees who work at the plant.

The trends in managing are toward closer and tighter control over operations. With computers able to process enormous amounts of data, management has available the means of obtaining finite measures of productivity, account for costs, and exercise tight control over individual work output. This move toward more sophisticated control is based on the assumption that it is management's reponsibility to compel better performance from the workforce.

This move toward control comes at a time when behavioral scientists are finding that what employees expect from work has changed, with the employees of today having work values which place importance upon the following:

Participation in decisions
Communication from management about what it is doing
Work that is challenging, interesting, and rewarding
Recognition of their contributions to the company
Compensation which reflects performance

Because of the need to obtain a superior return from the company's investment in its human resources, an appropriate style of managing for the plant will include recognition of contemporary employee values and sound management of the human resource.

To operationalize this concept of managing, a statement of operating philosophy such as the one which follows has been developed for the plant.

Operating Philosophy for the Plant

The management philosophy of this plant is based on the knowledge that employees are the largest nonfinancial resource which the company can utilize in achieving its business objectives. The way in which the company manages its human resource can materially affect the profitability of this facility and its attractiveness as a place to work. Therefore, we base our management practices on these important assumptions:

• The company will achieve its business goals if all employees participate in the process of setting operating goals, and if management responds to employee ideas and suggestions about better ways of working together which have the result of improving business performance.

• Employee concerns are management's concerns, and management will actively seek information from employees for the purpose of quickly identifying and reacting to complaints and problems in the organization which may hinder our ability to work together to achieve business objectives.

• This organization must be innovative, and provide creative, interesting, and challenging jobs for employees so that people can develop their skills and abilities in this company, and so the company can respond quickly to changes in business conditions.

• Employees are paid for performance. Performance of employees shall be a major determinant in employee compensation, with management providing systems which tie increased pay as directly as possible to increased performance.

Because of these beliefs, management of this facility intends to use a style of managing which is based essentially on those elements which exist in smoothly functioning teams of people.

The company intends that every person, given his or her level of responsibility and technical capabilities, will have input to the problem-solving process as appropriate, because the company believes that individuals are in the best position to assess production needs in their areas of responsibility. The company believes that the efficiency of production will suffer if people are not consulted or asked for their contributions.

Although management is ultimately responsible for the successful operation of the plant, decision making cannot be viewed as the sole right or obligation of management. The company believes that each person must make decisions moment by moment as the need arises, and company management wishes to involve employees in decisions that affect them.

The function of the plant's management is to make this style of management happen so that the organization's human resources can be used in a superior manner to attain the company's business objectives and provide an excellent place in which to work.

Responsibilities of Management and Employees

Consistent with the assumptions and statements of management philosophy detailed in the preceding section of this document, it is appropriate to detail the respective responsibilities of management and employees. This statement of what is expected of employees and what management commits to do is critical to establishing understanding and trust between management and employees. It also represents a rather dramatic departure from traditional management approaches, where management is seen as being responsible for everything, including business results, and where employees are chiefly responsible for doing what management says. In the plant, both management and employees share responsibilities for making the plant a success. Management's responsibilities include the following:

1. Management will provide a safe working environment for employees. While employees are obligated to bring safety questions and problems to the attention of management, it is management's responsibility to take necessary and aggressive actions to provide a safe work environment and to assess the safety implications of changes in the work environment. This includes instances when new machinery is installed, new chemicals or substances are introduced into the manufacturing process, and new employees are added to the workforce.

2. Management is responsible for operationalizing the concept and spirit of the management style as outlined in the statement of plant operating philosophy. This includes a responsibility for ensuring that managers new to the plant are thoroughly instructed in the concepts and behaviors necessary to manage in the plant.

3. Management is responsible for ensuring that the plant is in compliance with federal, state, and local regulations with regard to equal employment opportunity, safety and environmental quality, wage and hour laws, the National Labor Relations Act, and other guidelines and statutes.

4. Management is responsible for maintaining ethical and legal conduct of the company's business, and employees can expect management not to expose the company or its employees to liability by virtue of violating antitrust regulations, generally accepted codes of business ethics, or conflicts of interest between employees and the company.

5. Management is responsible for providing the leadership, capital resources, tools and equipment, staff services, management techniques and systems, human resources, and control mechanisms necessary to encourage innovative and productive ideas, become aware of and react to problems, and attain the plant's business objectives.

6. Management of the plant is responsible to Donaldson Company management for the successful and profitable operation of the plant. While management of the plant will actively seek to use employee inputs in decision making, management is ultimately responsible to the larger company for timely and proper management decisions, actions, and controls necessary to operate the plant.

The plant's operating style incorporates significant participation from its employees. The employees share in the success of the business, are encouraged to help the plant achieve, and receive the reward of financial gain, job security, and an excellent work environment. In order to maintain this type of working relationship between management and employees, the employees are expected to accept responsibility for assisting management in the attainment of the plant's operating objectives. Included in the responsibilities of employees are the following:

1. Employees are responsible for helping to formulate and for following safety rules and common health and safety practices designed to protect employees. This includes a responsibility for using protective equipment designed for or provided for a particular company operation.

2. Employees are responsible for coming to work promptly, regularly, and agreeably. Attendance is expected of all employees, and management expects that absenteeism for causes other than illness, accident, or extenuating circumstance is within the control of employees.

3. Employees are responsible for actively participating in the successful operation of the plant. This includes generating ideas and suggestions which can benefit the operation. In addition, em-

ployees are expected to communicate to management their positions on problems which affect the plant's operation.

4. Employees are responsible for collaborating with management on plant business issues, participating in decision making, and following through on decisions which they are to implement.

These broad statements of mutual expectancy are designed to be communicated to all members of plant management and all employees in the facility. They are appropriately discussed in interviews of prospective employees, and again as part of a new employee's orientation.

Predicted Outcomes of the Human-Resource-Oriented Approach to Managing

The decision to utilize the style of managing described in this document is based upon a conclusion that to do so makes good business sense, rather than simply being a recognition of a need to provide good employee relations programs.

Implementation of the policies and practices described in this document will require significant time, management involvement, personal energy, and management resources, and will require a commitment to long-range paybacks for today's investment of management time. The returns for this investment are great, however, and management can expect to achieve benefits in terms of both operating and management results. These results should be as follows:

Operating results
   High production output beginning during plant start-up.
   High quality of the finished products.
   A lowered direct labor cost.
   Reduced waste and scrap.

Management results
   Low turnover in the workforce.
   An acceptably low level of absenteeism.

The ability to attract good, productive employees.
Maintenance of nonunion statue

Supporting Policy Areas Necessary to Implement Management's Philosophy

To operationalize the preceding management philosophy, this section details a number of important policy areas which are keys to successful human resource management. The list is not all-inclusive, and, as with any start-up venture, the start-up of the plant will undoubtedly provide challenges in areas of human resource management not covered here. Continued creativity and adaptation will be required as the plant progresses through its first months and years of operation.

The listing which follows is deliberately briefly defined, with the final details to be derived from discussion among the management staff, and with the anticipation that changes and modification will be necessary over time to fit the changing needs of the business and the employees.

Staffing practices

There are several key elements necessary for successful staffing of the plant. First, management must think through and plan the hiring process in detail to attract the best employees for the plant.

The understanding of what the company is really like begins for employees when they begin work on their first day of employment. But management's style can have a desirable effect much earlier in the hiring process. That effect really starts at the point when the potential employee first becomes aware of the company's presence in the job marketplace. Everything the employee learns, reads, or hears from others influences his feelings toward, and understanding of, what it will be like to work in the plant.

It is critical, therefore, that management plan the hiring process in detail to be certain that at every point in the hiring process, potential employees are hearing, seeing, and receiving appropriate messages about work life at the plant. A required step is for management to meet prior to starting the initial hiring cycle to discuss ways of making the best impression on potential employees, and deciding how to manage the hiring process from initial communications through interviewing, reference checking, hiring, and orientation.

Another key element is that selection criteria be established so that the company hires only those employees likely to meet management's expectancies. A substantial portion of employee turnover, absenteeism, workers' compensation costs, and "pro-union" biases can be traced to certain key employee attitude and background factors. Certain methods of avoiding such performance problems are discussed elsewhere in this document. The selection process can be used as a way to hire plant personnel who are likely to best benefit the Donaldson Company in the long run.

Certain general criteria for selecting the "best" employees for the plant are provided as a framework. After a six-month period it will be possible to assess the link between these criteria and the performance of employees hired. Following such an analysis, specific criteria for selection can be developed which account for all the specific needs of the plant.

The following list of key factors for selecting production employees is rank-ordered in terms of those most important. These factors should *not* be used when selecting plant personnel for "fast track" movement or key management jobs, or when attempting to select "high potential" employees.

Of those employees applying for plant jobs, preferential treatment should be given to the following candidates (rank-ordered in terms of importance):

1. Applicants with no union membership background.
2. Applicants from the local labor market.
3. Applicants with the lowest skills, but still having the skills necessary to meet minimum job requirements.

4. Applicants who fall generally within the 35- to 45-year age range (as a rule, the older the applicants, the more likely they are to stay with their jobs).
5. Applicants with a minimum of formal education, but who still have the necessary education to meet minimum job requirements.
6. Applicants who are married (the longer the marriage, the more likely the applicants are to be stable in terms of job mobility).
7. Applicants with one or two children (if necessary, choose applicants with any number of children rather than no children).

(Additionally, research supports the selection of applicants who display values which tend toward the more traditional side. The interviewing process can be used to isolate candidates in terms of their value preferences.)

Finally, all applicants should have a thorough reference check before an offer is made. This check must minimally include a determination of the applicant's past turnover, absenteeism, and health history, as well as his length of prior job service in each of his past jobs, and the actual reasons for leaving his employers.

As an outcome of the hiring procedures, those employed must represent the minority and female composition of the community. A start-up situation gives management the opportunity to preclude EEO problems through a thorough analysis of skills available in the local labor market, and supporting hiring practices which replicate as closely as possible the makeup of the community in terms of minorities and females for all labor categories. If minorities and females are not readily available in certain job categories, especially skilled crafts, management, and professional categories, current EEO requirements hold management responsible for assessing those who have the greatest potential to perform such jobs from the available pool of females or minorities, and providing accelerated development so that the company makes every effort to provide minority or female representation in all job categories.

Compensation

Pay practices in the plant are based on a simply stated principle: "We Pay for Performance." To operationalize this statement, pay practices are as much as possible based on total plant performance with appropriate attention paid to competitive rates of pay by other area employees.

Community wage averages are used as a comparison, and wage surveys are used as a measure of competitiveness. These surveys, taken on an annual basis, will provide a basis for comparing base wage rates between the plant and other area employers. Surveys need to be sufficiently detailed to accumulate information concerning average straight-time hourly wages, shift differentials, types of products, plant size, union status, and other distinguishing characteristics significant for comparison.

A desirable posture is for the plant to maintain a base wage rate above the 50th percentile of area employers. The effects of the plant productivity sharing plan is not to be included in the comparisons. This allows employee contributions toward increased productivity to be above the company's commitment to pay competitively with the area average.

Salaried status

Because of the company's desire to encourage a participative and collaborative relationship between management and employees, all employees have "salaried" status in the plant. This means there are no time clocks, time cards, or other symbolic differences between groups of employees. Employees are still classified as either "exempt" or "nonexempt" as required by federal law to distinguish jobs in the plant which are entitled to overtime payment under specifications of the law. In addition, there are record-keeping requirements for reporting hours worked consistent with this law. Other than this distinction, the intent of the policy is that all employees enjoy the same rights and privileges regardless of level in the organization. For production employees, this means that they participate in a standard sick leave program also offered to management, they are offered employee benefits designed for salaried employees, and they enjoy the privilege of paid absences for personal or family illness.

The company provides this salaried status to employees because it believes employees will act responsibly when given fair treatment. As with all other management systems and practices at the plant, this extension of salaried status to all employees must be carefully managed to discourage abuses by any employee or group of employees. Appropriate discipline procedures are available to provide management with control over abuses of the freedoms associated with salaried status. It is expected that management control will be applied consistently to both management and nonmanagement personnel.

Benefits

In addition to a salary, the company provides a benefits package to employees. At the plant, because of the all-salaried status of employees, the benefit levels are the same for all employees. In this way the company can include the largest numbers of employees in insured group plans for greatest economy, and offer the same basic benefits package to employees at all levels in the organization.

Benefit levels will be determined through surveys of area benefits practice, with primary emphasis being placed on remaining competitive with the plant area. In addition the company plan offerings and benefits levels will be consistent with other Donaldson locations.

Development

The company intends to develop the talent needed for future business growth from within the plant when possible, to obtain personnel from other Donaldson plants as a secondary source, and to hire from outside the company as a final source of talent.

In addition, management is responsible for developing the

skills of internal people to make them attractive and prepared to accept challenging assignments at other company locations. Given these objectives, development of employees is one of management's highest priorities with the focus of development being on helping employees perform their present jobs successfully, and preparing them to accept increasing job responsibilities in the future. The orientation of new employees is to be used as a first step in the development process. Orientation is the responsibility of the employee's immediate supervisor. A well-conducted orientation process can have a positive and long-lasting impact on new employees. At this point in their careers, employees are highly dependent on management for information, and management has the opportunity to subtly reinforce the employee's choice of the plant as a place to work.

Providing a booklet with written statements of management philosophies, plant rules, descriptions of benefit plans, information on the business, and other items is a preferred means of demonstrating to employees management's commitment to a continuing process of development for employees.

Training

Managers and supervisors occupy key roles in the plant. Because of the management style established for the plant, it is critical that individuals who direct the work of others manage consistently. It is also critical that all supervisors and managers as a group manage in a way that is consistent with one another.

To achieve this consistency, all those in supervisory and managerial positions must be given adequate training in the desired management skills early in their careers with the company. Ideally managers and supervisors should attend a management training program prior to being assigned to jobs where they are asked to direct others.

Because the realities of organizational life will often preclude the opportunity to plan such training for all new supervisors, it would be acceptable if new supervisors attend a supervisory training program within the first 60 days of their assignment to a supervisory job.

Department managers are to attend a specialized training program aimed at developing their interpersonal managing skills within one year after assuming their management positions.

Operator training

The responsibility for training operatives is to be shared between supervisors and the new employee's peers. The employee's peers are the primary source of information about the functioning of the work group and the details of how to perform a specific job. Management's responsibilities include an overall orientation to the organization, and the providing of information about company policies, programs, and mechanisms for communicating with management. This process is designed to ensure that the employee's performance increases to a productive level in the shortest possible period of time.

Advancement

It is the policy of the plant to move employees laterally for career growth, to offer internal job opportunities to employees before going outside the organization to hire, and to organize a method of formally posting job opportunities available for employees to bid on as a means for individuals to advance their own careers.

Decision making

The management style of the plant encourages participation of individual employees and groups of employees in major decisions affecting the operation of the plant. Some experiments in group decision making have proved to be failures, with operating management feeling it was managing in an environment where "the inmates were running the asylum." To prevent such an occurrence in the plant, but to preserve the principle that group decisions can be better than individual decisions, these parameters are drawn for decision making in the plant:

- The plant manager is accountable for operating results to Donaldson Company management.
- The plant manager holds the management staff accountable for operating results.
- The style of managing actively solicits ideas, suggestions, and participation in decisions, especially on the part of employees who will be most directly affected by implementation of the decision.
- The plant manager's staff is to function as a productive, decision-making, and problem-solving team, and will collaborate on issues of major importance to the successful operation of the facility.

Communications

In an environment such as the one created for the plant, communication and information flow have a special importance. The management style in the plant both permits and encourages upward, downward, and horizontal communications. The vehicles for communication include the following:

- Meetings to be held each month to discuss business results. These meetings are intended to be short, perhaps 30 minutes in length.
- Attitude surveys to be conducted after the initial plant start-up, again when plant size increases by 50%, or at intervals of 18 months.
- An employee publication or house organ distributed to employees. (The corporate newspaper can be used as a medium, or the plant can tailor its communications to employees by assembling articles from the corporate paper, along with locally written articles, into a plant publication which features timely news about the plant.)

- Articles about the plant which appear in the corporate paper. (Such articles should feature plant employees, and be distributed throughout the Donaldson organization.)
- A formalized process to handle employee suggestions and complaints. The major objectives of the complaint/suggestion process is to:
  1. Get at the actual complaint or define the specifics of the employee's suggestion.
  2. Encourage employees to use this channel of upward communication.
  3. Accomplish the first two objectives with the support of supervision, and, in the case of complaints, to maintain the morale of supervisors.

The complaint/suggestion system is based upon the principle of an open-door policy but with a more closely defined structure. The policy is designed to allow employees to:

1. Talk to their supervisors first.
2. Speak with their functional or department manager.
3. Speak directly with the plant manager for resolution if they are not satisfied.

The plant manager's decision is to be accepted as final. The form on the following page is an example of one that can be used or adapted for use at the plant.

Structure

Questions about how the organization should be structured will depend on the stage of business growth, the plant and management group size, and other factors that will be identified by management in the course of running the plant. In general, these elements will guide the decisions about organizational structure:

- A span of 5–7 direct reports will be maintained for plant manager and department managers.
- The production supervisor position is to be chartered as the

EMPLOYEE SUGGESTION/COMPLAINT
PROCEDURE

Your supervisor is responsible for listening to your suggestions and for trying to resolve your work-related problems. However, there may be times when you are not entirely satisfied with his response to your suggestion or solution to your problem. You may want to appeal your case to someone else. This procedure establishes the way you may do just that:

STEP 1

The problem or suggestion should be discussed with your supervisor to give him an opportunity to understand the facts of the situation or the nature of your suggestion. We expect that most problems can be resolved after a full discussion of the facts; however, if you are not satisfied, you may take your suggestion or complaint to step 2.

In cases of unusual plantwide situations or "personal" conditions between you and your supervisor, you may not want to discuss the problem or your suggestion with your immediate supervisor. You have the choice of taking the problem or suggestion directly to the plant manager, who will assist you in these cases.

STEP 2

Your problem or suggestion will then be heard and discussed with you by your functional or department manager. If you are still not satisfied, you may wish to go to step 3.

STEP 3

You may again have the opportunity to discuss the problem or suggestion with the plant manager if you wish. After this discussion the plant manager's decision will be considered final.

Because it is important that employee ideas, suggestions, and complaints receive prompt attention, the following time limit has been established for providing you a response:

Step 1   5 working days
Step 2   5 working days
Step 3 10 working days

At any level of the organization, we are willing to hear your thoughts, suggestions, and problems.

critical human resource management position, with a blend of technical expertise and management skill required.

- The organization's structure should be reviewed through a formal analysis when the workforce changes by 50%. The analysis should involve a review of current business objectives, the numbers of people in each functional area, and an assessment of the functional relationships required to manage the operation successfully.

- In addition to the formal organization, heavy emphasis is placed on informal relationships to allow maximum input to decision making, communications, and participation by appropriate employees regardless of organizational relationships.

Operating objectives

Operating goals are to be established and communicated throughout the plant. The specific measures attached to these goals are to be a product of agreement among the management staff, and based on prior discussions with operating employees. The goals are to be prioritized and should include goals related to:

Production
Quality
Safety
Cost Management
Profitability
Social Responsibility
Manpower Management

Productivity improvement

Increases in productivity are to be the result of collaborative efforts of management and employees. To encourage the attainment of productivity goals, the company agrees to share equally with employees the gains in productivity accomplished by these joint efforts.

The details of the productivity sharing for the plant go beyond the scope of this document, but the system is to be designed to achieve four major outcomes:

- A sustained and measurable increase in plant productivity over time.
- The application of individual and collective employee ideas and suggestions to boost production output.
- The active involvement and interest of employees in the success of the company.
- A lessened vulnerability to unionization.

The elements of a suitable productivity sharing plan for the plant will be the product of professional analysis and design, but will include the following:

- Base productivity measurement based on measures of past productivity, productivity in other, similar plants, or engineering estimates of output capacity translated into the hour value of output compared with total hours worked by the group.
- A defined group of employees will share in the gains in productivity.
- Productivity will be shared equally between employees and the company.
- No attempt will be made to pinpoint whether employees or management created the savings.
- The system will allow for technological or capital improvements, addition of new products, and addition of new employees.
- The system will provide a cap on the productivity payout to prevent runaway production.

Work climate

It is the responsibility of management to provide an environment in which all employees can productively work together to meet personal and organizational goals. "Work climate" is the term used to describe this elusive quality in an organization; although difficult to define, it differentiates a good place to work from a poor one.

The nature of the desired work climate for the plant will be a subject for plant management to discuss during the early weeks and months of the plant's operations. It is probably easiest to discuss in terms of providing an answer to these questions:

> What is it like for employees to work in this plant?
> What are we doing that makes this a good place to work?
> How are employees reacting to our management actions?

There are more complex questions which management will wish to ask, and the answers will not be easy to get, nor to accept at times, even when obtained. But three elements provide the basis for establishing the work climate in the plant and there are systematic ways of assessing management's success in developing a desirable work climate, as follows:

- Providing a safe work environment as outlined in the section of this document dealing with management responsibilities—this is a central responsibility of management.
- Providing an environment which is conducive to effect teamwork—defined as work groups or departments working effectively as units to solve problems and contribute to the profitable operation of the plant.
- Providing systems, programs, and practices in which management responds to ideas, suggestions, and complaints.

Management's performance with regard to establishing this desired work climate is measurable through the use of periodic surveys of employee attitudes. The results of such surveys can serve as useful tools to formulate changes in management practices, as well as to assess the success of present and past practices.

Performance management

Performance management as a concept goes beyond traditional performance appraisal and relates employee performance to measurable objectives, as well as to the company's systems of reward and recognition for performance. The concept of performance is applied to the plant manager, department heads, and first-line supervisors. Nonsupervisory professional and technical employees are also included, but production workers are not. The performance management plan consists of the following:

• Measurable standards of performance are to be established jointly by the plant manager and individual department heads. Likewise, standards are established by agreement between department heads and supervisory, professional, or technical personnel. These standards are to be well communicated.

• Standards are to include operating and human resource objectives.

• An annual personal evaluation is to be conducted for covered employees, at which time performance against standard is to be a central issue of discussion.

• The company's performance appraisal form can serve as a basis for conducting and documenting this evaluation.

• Development planning for each individual being evaluated will be done at the same time.

• Performance of the entire plant in terms of human resource and operating objectives serves as a basis for review for the plant manager.

The outcome of the performance management process includes:

• Recognition of the individual contributions employees have made toward meeting previously set standards.

- Coaching and counseling employees to help them attain increased results in the future.
- Thorough discussion and understanding by both parties of the results that were not attained.
- Establishment of new or revised standards for the next review period, including agreement on resources, development, or modifications necessary to permit the attainment of objectives.
- An understanding by the person being reviewed of those behaviors necessary to perform in a superior fashion.
- An understanding by the reviewer of the rated person's interests in career growth, as well as an agreement on development plans to be implemented in the next 12 months.

Subsequent pay increases will reflect employee performance as managed under this program.

Maintenance of nonunion status

The style of managing formulated for the plant is designed to provide the good working conditions, good wages and benefits, fair treatment, and personal respect that employees seek in their jobs. Properly executed, this managing style will preclude feelings on the part of employees that a union can offer advantages over current company management practices. The maintenance of nonunion status is based on the following assumptions:

- Management accepts that one of the plant's objectives is to maintain nonunion status.
- A substantial portion of the cause for unionization can be traced to negative employee attitudes resulting from inappropriate management practices.
- Unionization is not inevitable, and the application of sound management practices and principles serves to significantly decrease vulnerability to it.
- The signing of union cards, the occurrence of union elections, and poor morale at the plant are clear indications that sound

management principles and practices are not being properly and consistently applied.

Donaldson is not anti-union, and the company's approaches to maintaining nonunion status are not based upon defensive, legalistic, or anti-union tactics. Rather, the company takes the position that effective human resource management and high-quality work environments can preclude the desire by employees to seek representation by unions or other third parties.

The company's experience has been that unionized workforces are more costly to the company, given the resultant lack of management flexibility, the costs of contract negotiation and administration, and the real potential for the disruption of operations due to strikes.

Maintaining nonunion status requires the acceptance of the following:

- Plant management at all levels is directly responsible for implementing employee relations policies and practices consistent with sound human resource management principles.
- All plant management and supervisory personnel are accountable for implementing these policies and practices in such a way as to preclude any attempt, on the part of the workforce, to seek representation by unions or any other third party.
- The corporate human resource function will assist plant management to ensure that employee relations policies and procedures are applied appropriately and consistently at the facility so as to make unnecessary any employee attempt to seek third-party representation.
- The plant management group is to develop a plan for maintaining nonunion status. This plan utilizes input from members of plant management and the corporate human resource function.
- The plan for maintaining nonunion status is to be communicated to employees in terms of management's plan for maintaining a healthy work climate in the plant.

- Each year plant management and representatives from the corporate human resource management function will meet to assess the plant's vulnerability to unionization. This assessment will focus on—

1. Facility climate as measured by
    Attitude surveys and union vulnerability indices.
    Interviews with employees or small group meetings.
    Actions taken in reaction to previous climate data.
2. Pay and benefits systems to determine if
    Systems are competitive with area practices.
    A relationship exists between pay and performance.
    Pay systems motivate employees.
    Employees are relatively satisfied with pay and benefits as compared with national counterparts.
3. Employee relations policies and procedures to determine if
    Policies and procedures are clearly communicated and understood by employees, and administered consistently.
    Revisions are needed in present policies, or if new ones need to be added.
4. Training, to examine
    The quantity, quality, and timeliness of training efforts.
    Whether training is targeted and applied in employee groups.
5. Communications, to evaluate
    The formal and informal communications systems, specifically with regard to the clarity and impact of communication.
    Employee understanding of and satisfaction with communications.
    The actual use of communications systems, especially the suggestion/complaint system.
6. A review of
    Steps taken since the preceding assessment.
    How well the facility's plan has been or is being implemented.

16

Organization behavior in the 1980s

As WE MOVE into the 1980s, the impact of modern technology on business is almost incalculable. Perhaps the most vivid symbol of technological change in the 1970s was the electronic revolution. Consider, for example, the calculator. Ten years ago the hand-held calculator was approximately the size of a cigar box and could do little more than add, subtract, multiply, and divide. A calculator fitting this description could be purchased for approximately $130. With inflation, that's the equivalent of more than $250 today. It is now possible to purchase a calculator that stores data and does exponents, roots, pi, and, of course, the basic arithmetical calculations for $15. And instead of being cigar-box size, today's calculator can fit into a coat pocket.

In the past decade, technology gave medical and military science new and more sophisticated tools with which to work. Technology gave education and business more powerful, versatile, and economical computers to buy and use. Yet the power of technology cannot be used to solve the most important problem faced by American business in the 1980s.

Alvin Toffler, in his new book, which he calls *The Third Wave,**

* New York: William Morrow, 1980.

presents a portrait of an emerging society that promises to change our methods of managing dramatically. Toffler reasons that the agricultural revolution that began over 10,000 years ago started what he describes as the *first wave* of historical change. The industrial revolution of 300 years ago produced a *second wave* of civilization that today is quickly giving way to a *third wave* that will revolutionize both family and corporate structures.

The second wave of civilization—the industrial society—brought with it a "code book" for everyday life. The code book identified standardization, maximization, and synchronization as guiding principles that could be applied to business, government, and daily life. Punctuality and scheduling have become the religious tenets of the second wave of civilization. Because of the need for conformity and standardization, daily life-styles were tied to a 9-to-5 work schedule. The rhythms of sleep and wakefulness, of work and play, had to conform to the fixed schedule of a job. Being on time for work and for appointments is inbred in the thinking of the second wave.

The new code book of the third wave of civilization attacks much of what the second-wave person was taught to believe. The third-wave person challenges the need for conformity, punctuality, standardization, and the efficiency of centralization. Toffler points to the emergence of flexitime (an arrangement that permits workers to select their own working hours within predetermined limits) and the increase in the number of night, part-time, and female workers as evidence that the third wave is already under way. The code book of the second wave, he reasons, has already been broken. More and more people are working outside the 9-to-5 schedule and consumer patterns are rapidly changing. Supermarkets, banks, and other businesses have had to change their work hours to serve night, flexitime, and part-time workers.

But the third wave springs from deeper changes than these more visible factors. Toffler notes that there are psychological, economic, and technological forces that are pushing us quickly toward a new civilization. The population has changed. People today are more educated and affluent than their parents. They also differ in terms of the work they do and the products they consume. They demand to be treated more as individuals and they resist socially imposed schedules.

In the 1980s we are sure to find organizations emphasizing efficiency, cost containment, and management selection and development. In previous chapters, I have outlined a number of behavioral science concepts and techniques that have proved successful in helping management achieve these ends. In this final chapter I have taken a forward glance at the future role of organization behavior by examining some key changes that organizations must make in their management practices in preparation for Toffler's third wave of civilization.

Professional and Management Education

The wide range of new technology that is moving into our lives in the form of home video recordings and computer communication systems promises to change the way organizations conduct their management training efforts. Computers have made it possible to conduct conferences or one-on-one discussions through electronic video information-exchange systems. Teleprinters and home video screens make it possible to communicate "face to face" at a time convenient to both parties.

As pressure for corporate profit mounts organizations will seek ways to analyze educational needs better, improve the efficiency of delivery systems, and design effective evaluation methods. As the educational level of employees continues to rise, "individualization," "tailoring," and "flexibility" will become key terms in the education lexicon. Educational programs that focus on the needs of individual employees will require major changes in the approach business takes toward professional and management education.

As newer approaches become available, formal courses will become a luxury. Computer-assisted instruction, with its emphasis on individual learning, and the emergence of home video cassettes and other technological innovations will make learning readily available to employees in the privacy of their offices or homes. Technology in the 1980s will make educational development an ongoing process. Education will continue throughout the employee's tenure with a company.

People trained in the behavioral sciences will be challenged to design reliable and valid methods for assessing educational needs and evaluating program results. Practitioners will also be required to act as liaisons with line management. The notion of selling educational programs to line management will become obsolete. Rather, staff specialists will have to understand business operations and management's organizational needs as a prerequisite for designing and/or providing educational services. Thus, the concept of bridging careers (placing staff specialists in line positions and vice versa) will be used with increasing regularity. Education specialists will be drawn from a pool of line managers and functional specialist positions.

Some companies have already begun to change their approaches to education and training dramatically. One company, for example, did a careful analysis of the rising cost associated with training management and supervisory personnel. They forecasted the costs of continuing to offer traditional classroom instruction for a five-year period. Their calculations indicated that the costs would soar at an average rate of over 20 percent each year to deliver programs that are widely used in company management education curriculums. They further concluded that traditional classroom instruction could meet only one-third of the company's educational requirements over a five-year period.

As a result of their analysis, they designed and are implementing a new approach to education that has thus far proved to be well received by top management and by participants. The approach they have taken employs the most up-to-date educational technology available at the current time. The technology has been organized around the concept of a central learning center. The learning center makes use of technology available through computer- and video-assisted instructions. The instructional programs available through the center cover such diverse areas as financial planning, chemistry, languages, general management principles, acquisition strategy, and a host of other programs that can be offered to employees on an individual or group basis. The center also makes use of video programs and other forms of self-instruction through individualized learning carrels. Participants can proceed at their own speed and at a time convenient to them.

But the learning center concept need not be geared exclusively to individual instruction. Educators from within the company, from universities, and from other professional organizations offering educational services can continue to conduct small and large classes using traditional methods or a combination of traditional and individualized instruction.

This educational approach has several advantages. First, it offers the best programs available on the market to management and supervisors at a time convenient to them. Second, it sharply reduces the costs of education associated with travel. Third, it reduces the costs associated with instructional time. Based on a cost-effectiveness analysis, the per-person instructional cost can be reduced by as much as 50 percent in the first year of operation.

The cost-effectiveness and convenience factors may not be the most important advantage of this approach. The fourth and perhaps most noteworthy benefit is that the approach allows for individual assessment. Before getting involved in the center, each participant can be provided with an analysis of his or her educational needs. An evaluation of progress can follow the completion of each program. Much of this kind of assessment is available through the technology offered in a learning center.

The fifth advantage is that the approach permits the organization to reach a far greater number of managers and supervisors. At least 40 percent more participants a year can be reached through this approach than can be reached through the traditional classroom approach—and at a substantially lower cost.

Since the approach allows for flexibility and for individual tailoring, the number of company employees required to operate a corporate educational program can be held to a minimum. The educational professionals employed by the company can then spend a greater percentage of their time developing programs for the center, assessing and evaluating training needs, and consulting individual employees. Their remaining time can be spent in an instructional role.

At a time in our history when more highly trained people are required than ever before, educational institutions are increasingly experiencing cost reductions and cutbacks in programs and personnel. How we as a nation will adapt to our need for education is not totally clear. No doubt the computer and other communication systems will play an increasing role. My own feeling is that private enterprise will also assume a greater responsibility for educating employees.

With the acceleration of technology our educational skills will quickly become obsolete. Added to this phenomenon is the fact that life expectancy is increasing, that the retirement age is now extended to 70, and that there is increasing pressure for employment policies now common in Europe. These factors will pose new challenges for management education practices. Alternatives to traditional education are a must for business if we are to continue to hold a competitive posture in the world market.

Management Succession and Development

During the 1980s business leadership will undergo great change. The generation of senior executives who entered business after World War II will be retiring. American industry will be faced with a critical shortage of general managers who have the background and experience necessary to manage at executive levels within the organization. With all the emphasis on management succession and development in the past two decades, hundreds of mid-sized and large corporations have still failed in their attempts to groom young executives to handle broad-based responsibilities. As a result, many companies are forced to go outside their organizations to find chief executives, senior vice-presidents, and divisional general managers. The cost of recruiting at this level is increasing rapidly. The cost of an executive search generally represents from 35 to 40 percent of an executive's salary in this country and up to 100 percent for overseas executives. Add to these fees the cost of relocating and the disruption caused when an interim manager must fill a vacated position. In many industries, such as steel, iron, and rubber, management has been so negligent in developing general managers in its middle management ranks that it faces serious problems in meeting the challenge of declining markets.

Yet executive management has recognized the need for management succession and development, as is evidenced by the increased numbers of positions in personnel departments that are supposedly responsible for helping corporations to plan systematically for future growth. In the 1970s new jobs and new departments were created for this express purpose.

It is quite common to see executive titles that include such phrases as human resource management, management development, or organization planning. Personnel executives are being pushed by top management to accelerate their efforts to develop and implement management succession programs. In a survey of over 300 personnel officers conducted in the summer of 1979, Haskell and Stein, an executive search firm, found that the vast majority named management succession planning as the most critical part of the personnel function in the 1980s.

The cost of good management development program promises to escalate even more in the 1980s unless companies consider alternative approaches. Formal management succession programs are expensive to develop and implement. The expense of hiring and maintaining professional managers and staff specialists to design career ladders, individual development programs, and a host of other human resource systems has been on the upswing for the past 10 or 15 years. Many succession programs require full-time employees at both the corporate and divisional levels. Furthermore, many plans cannot be implemented without substantial changes in organizational structure or job design. Even more importantly, most programs are ineffective because line management lacks the understanding of and commitment to management development.

In the future both top management and divisional executives must begin to accept the notion that selecting, developing, and promoting managers must become part of every manager's responsibility. To have a cost-effective and practical approach the responsibility for management succession and development must shift from a staff function to a line function.

The shift of responsibilities is, in fact, already occurring in some organizations. One large corporation, for example, has created functional committees, chaired by a top-management committee member, that assume responsibility for overseeing staffing and career development activities for five functional areas: marketing, manufacturing and engineering, research and development, finance, and human resources. The purpose of each of these five programs is to provide the corporation with professionals and executives of quality and skill through strategic recruitment and selection of candidates, detailed planning of position changes, and promotional progress for people who demonstrate high levels of performance.

Each committee meets on a quarterly basis and, with the help of organization behavior specialists, works on such matters as:

Establishing selection criteria for people who will be hired
Identifying and/or creating key positions toward which to plan interdivisional moves
Detailing plans to match people with available assignments and company needs
Establishing new positions or redesigning existing positions to provide growth opportunities for employees to meet short- and long-term business objectives

In this company line managers from each major functional area are given the responsibility and accountability for designing, initiating, and coordinating all management succession and development programs. This approach has the following advantages. First, it heightens the awareness within the organization of the importance of management development to the long- and short-term business needs of the company. Second, it forces incumbent managers to focus their goals on preparing the company for tomorrow as well as on achieving profits today. Third, it gives managers who normally make decisions on selection, development, and interdivisional moves a first-hand look at the strategies, techniques, programs, and costs used by personnel professionals in planning for succession and development.

A fourth advantage of this approach is that it prevents organizations from repeating the mistakes of the past wherein line management, faced with recession or the threat of recession, would freeze hiring and begin cutting back on management development programs. With line management closely involved with the company's succession and development efforts, the commitment to management development goals is equal to its commitment to other business goals.

Most companies need to know from three to five years in advance what their management needs will be at all levels. Personnel researchers operating from sophisticated demand forecast models have been only moderately successful in some organizations in predicting future management needs. With line management fully involved in people forecasting as well as sales forecasting, sophisticated statistical procedures, although helpful, are no longer necessary. Thus, another advantage of this approach is that it allows the organization to forecast its management's requirements regularly on the basis of data supplied by functional managers throughout the corporation.

A last advantage of transferring management succession and development to line managers is that it permits sophisticated programs to operate with only a minimum number of personnel professionals. Instead of assuming responsibility for all the programs associated with selection, development, and internal placement, the personnel professional acts only as educator and coordinator. Only a few professionals at the corporate level are needed instead of a large department of human resource personnel.

Labor Relations

The startling realization will surface in the 1980s that management, labor, and government must join together to find workable alternatives to the threat–counterthreat mentality that pervades company and labor negotiations. In response to the decline of American products and prestige in the world marketplace, new approaches to labor relations must be designed by those trained in the behavioral sciences.

If the United States is to solve its productivity problems, traditional approaches to labor relations must be abandoned and replaced by organization behavior approaches that focus more on the quality of work/life issues and mutual productivity goals. To accomplish this objective, companies and unions can begin by keeping regular tabs on worker attitudes toward productivity. Several companies have begun to do this by asking employees how productive they feel they are in their current assignment, using the productivity index discussed in Chapter 14.

The broad questions of productivity improvement, worker job satisfaction, safety, environmental protection, and other quality of work/life issues must be addressed collectively by labor, government, and management. Problem-solving, decision-making, and action-planning methods can serve as effective vehicles for conducting discussions led by behavioral specialists. Unions can take advantage of the strategies and techniques of the behavioral sciences by employing organization behavior practitioners within their ranks. The contributions of the behavorial sciences to the labor relations field could result in a change of normative behavior within and between government, labor, and management.

The principles related to building effective teamwork and improving employee productivity have particular relevance to the issues related to union and management relations. The question of how to improve relations with unions needs to be addressed as much by organization behavior practitioners as by union relations personnel.

Restructuring the Planning and Analytical Functions

One area of vital concern to executive management will be that of strategic planning and organizational structure. To gain maximum efficiency from the human resources employed, top management will depend more and more on professionals who are trained to study organizational structure as it relates to the overall strategic plan of the corporation and its operating units.

Many of today's top-flight executives realize the importance of tying structure to strategy. Yet in most corporations, business planning functions are separate from organization planning functions. Too often, the chief executive officer works independently with the company's top business planner and top human resource executive. In order to achieve optimum results departments specializing in planning the company's human resource future must move toward integration with other planning and analytical functions.

In Chapters 2, 3, and 4 I outlined an approach that can be taken by management to increase the effectiveness of its planning efforts. The tasks required to gain this effectiveness can be facilitated by designing an organizational function that merges human resource planning research with other functions that use similar analytical processes and address similar organizational issues. The rapid growth of human resource professionals from approximately 43,000 in the early 1960s to an estimated 430,000 in the early 1980s, together with an accelerated growth of other planning functions, has created much duplication of effort. Many personnel departments, for example, are staffed to run their own personnel management information systems, quite separate from other management information systems.

Merging the analytical and planning functions into a more centralized function can facilitate the interaction between disciplines and create multicareer paths for staff professionals. More importantly, however, such a merger will provide executive management with a broader, more reliable information base for decision making. Decisions to acquire or diversify should be made by organization analysts and management development specialists along with market researchers and other business analysts. The analysis of operating problems (productivity, efficiency, safety, and so on) should be made by organization behavior analysts as well as operations researchers and financial analysts. Behavioral information specialists as well as computer and financial specialists should have input into the design of company management information systems.

Integrating the planning and analytical functions through organizational structure is both logical and practical. You can only manage a profitable organization by doing a better job of collecting, analyzing, and synthesizing information.

Changing Organizational Structures

Today's competitive business climate has forced many companies into an almost perpetual state of reorganization. Decentralization—giving the company's operating divisions as much decision making as possible—has become almost a theology for many top executives. Management consulting firms specializing in reorganization are employed to break departments in larger companies down to more autonomous "profit centers." In the late 1970s the profit-center concept became the new management buzz word to describe the notion of shifting decision making to lower organizational levels.

While decentralization has become popular in management

circles, another, parallel, phenomenon has taken place. Corporate financial functions are growing larger because of increased centralization of control. Top management has recognized the need to increase the analytical and planning capabilities of financial functions and has positioned these functions high enough in the organization to permit professional finance personnel ease of movement up, down, and across hierarchical lines of authority. Their reporting relationship, together with their data collection capabilities, provides them with a base of power that allows them to exert a lot of influence on the executive decision-making process.

The question of how to organize—what to centralize, what to decentralize—will present a difficult challenge to top management in the 1980s. The sociology and psychology of the 1970s urged people to look inward, discover themselves, and manage their own destiny. The social cry of the 1980s promises to emphasize the need for even more individual involvement and decision making.

Although decentralization and other forms of organizational schemes, such as matrixing (discussed in Chapter 6), address some of the issues associated with decision making, they cannot be used as simple solutions to the issues associated with organizing for optimum results. Establishing profit centers may be helpful to some organizations, but the fact remains that not all functions should be decentralized. More than ever, top management needs regular independent input on matters related to law, research and development, finance, planning, and human resources from highly trained personnel. In most instances it is unwise to break these functional areas into decentralized units.

As I pointed out in Chapter 5, there is no formula that leads to a "best way" of organizing a business. The principles that might be applied to organizing a profit center do not necessarily apply to staff functions. The organization behavior professional can serve an extremely important role in helping top management design organizational structures that are tailored to the business needs of the corporation. In the 1980s it will be necessary to find new ways to organize the company's human resources. Professionals in the field of organization behavior should lead the way.

Tomorrow's organizational structures will necessarily be centralized and hierarchical, for maximum efficiency and control. At the same time, organizations will need new patterns of structure that are unlike any of our present forms. The behavioral sciences must begin to lead the way in finding these new patterns.

The Human Resource Audit

For many years, companies have relied on professional organizations and internal staff personnel to conduct regular audits of company financial and operating practices. In some instances audits are only fact-finding tools that help management assess performance or identify areas in which further investigation may be warranted. In other instances audits provide management with recommendations on specific changes for correcting the deficiencies they have revealed.

There are sharp differences of opinion as to how an audit function should be used within an organization, but there is general agreement that auditing serves a valuable purpose in assuring management that its objectives are being carried out. There is even further argument that an audit should identify the financial or operational conditions that are capable of being improved. To be successful, auditing must be conducted regularly and systematically against predetermined corporate or industry standards. To maintain maximum objectivity, an audit should be conducted by personnel outside of the work unit being audited. The practice of auditing company operations has become a formal activity with a distinctive work content.

In much the same way, organizations should begin a regular audit of their personnel practices. For the most part, top management is unaware of the potential savings in efficiency and in real dollars that can be realized by streamlining day-to-day personnel practices. Let's examine an example of this potential.

In recent years, many companies have reorganized their purchasing functions in such a way that there is strong central control.

The rationale for greater centralization is that the company can gain greater leverage in its dealings with suppliers. The same rationale can be applied to the procurement of human resources. In most large companies hiring is done in a decentralized manner. Local personnel specialists deal with employment agencies, advertise for jobs, and interview candidates. The hiring process is only as good as the personnel specialist. Rarely, if ever, is his or her efficiency ever measured. Yet the professional who specializes in hiring knows that it is possible to control such things as advertising costs, interview-to-hire ratios, and employment fees.

Auditing hiring practices and centralizing for greater control can lead to substantial savings in employment costs. One mid-sized company of 4,000 employees cut its hiring costs by more than $600,000 in one year by first auditing its hiring practices and then redesigning its recruiting and employment procedures.

Auditing training and development costs, compensation and benefits practices, formal communications programs, labor relations approaches, affirmative action guidelines and practices, and other human resource activities can produce great cost savings for a corporation. A regular annual personnel audit will also compel human resource executives to improve the quality of their people and their services.

Organizations can go outside the corporation and employ a professional management consulting firm or they can conduct their own audits. If they do their own audit, management can form an audit team consisting of corporate and divisional specialists who are highly trained in their respective areas of expertise. In larger organizations the audit team may become a permanent body with full-time responsibilities. In medium-sized or smaller companies, the audit team might function as a temporary, part-time body.

As the costs of selecting, compensating, training, retaining, and promoting personnel continue to escalate at an alarming rate, organizations must find more innovative approaches to personnel management. The audit is a vital first step in the process of gaining control, exercising leverage, and reducing costs in the personnel function.

Summary

Textbooks and articles written in the 1970s on subjects related to organization behavior consistently reasoned that if companies were to remain competitive, they must continually renew themselves. The wave of renewal theory and practice that emerged exhorts organizations to alter structures, change policies, and experiment with new management behavior styles in order to respond more appropriately to changing times.

The renewal theme is supported by an overused yet important truism that science applied to technology has produced changes in organizational life that are diverse, complex, and revolutionary. The emergence of our society from an agricultural, pastoral, and rural heritage to one that is industrial, urban, and technological has been accompanied by new values, new reasons to interact, new demands, and new questions about the meaning and aim of life. Organizations have not merely responded to these changes; they have helped create them.

Critics of organizations have argued that bureaucracy does not permit personal growth, that it suffocates creativity and produces dull, robotlike pesonalities whose goal is conformity and adherence to policy. Concerned about the ultimate evaluation of bureaucracy, Max Weber, himself a prime developer of the theory of bureaucracy, leveled this criticism: "It is horrible to think that the world could one day be filled with nothing but little cogs, little men clinging to little jobs and striving toward bigger ones...." Weber feared that bureaucracy would produce men "who need order and nothing but order, who become nervous and cowardly if for one moment this order wavers...."*

---

* *An Intellectual Portrait.* Garden City, N.Y.: Doubleday, 1960.

At the time he wrote (in the late 1800s), Weber could not envision the many forces of change that have emerged in the past 50 years with a loud cry of opposition to his dreaded state of bureaucracy. Organizations have changed. In some instances they have renewed themselves as new challenges have confronted them.

This book has outlined a number of practical steps that can be taken to encourage further renewal. It argues for new planning, organizing, and managing approaches. And it demonstrates how the evaluation of an organization can be hastened and shaped by the science and technology of organization behavior. Organizations, whether they be mass production complexes or service industries, are intended as goal-attainment units. To survive, they must maintain internal control through effective management practices. To prosper, they must continually adapt to external change. To better mankind, they must help shape the destiny of our world.

Index